GOLF—MY SLICE OF LIFE

GOLF—MY SLICE OF LIFE

TED RAY

Illustrated by DAVID LANGDON

With an Introduction by DAI REES, CBE

W H ALLEN
LONDON & NEW YORK
A division of Howard & Wyndham
1972

Filmset in Photon Imprint 12 on 12½ pt. by
Richard Clay (The Chaucer Press) Ltd,
Bungay, Suffolk
and printed in Great Britain by
Fletcher & Son Ltd, Norwich
for the publishers
W H Allen Ltd, 43 Essex Street, London WC2R 3JG

Bound by
Richard Clay (The Chaucer Press) Ltd,
Bungay, Suffolk

ISBN 0 491 00891 0

This book is dedicated to the brave and ever-optimistic
golfers of the world, who have yet to break 100.
If each one bought a copy, I would be a millionaire!

CONTENTS

Dedication 5

Foreword 9

Introduction 11

1. It's only a game 13
2. On reducing one's handicap 16
3. Clobber 20
4. The perfect shot 22
5. The Achilles heel—or toe! 26
6. A strange happening 31
7. Where it really counts 35
8. Sydney 40
9. The gipsy life 43
10. The straight left arm 46
11. What's in a name? 49
12. The 'Humpers' 53
13. The Yorkshire terrier 57
14. Lessons from the top 62
15. The 'weaker' sex 67
16. The road to Maidenhead 71
17. 'Pro–Am' golf 75
18. Eccentrics and divot-takers (odds and sods!) 81
19. 'Blind' holes 85
20. Keep your head down and never change the size of your hat! 88
21. The missing links 90
22. Who said that? 93
23. Can we find a fourth? 98
24. Who says lightning never strikes twice? 101
25. Face to face 105
26. The stag party 110
27. 'Show-biz' golf 116
28. The Nineteenth—plus one 127

FOREWORD

For better or worse, this book is all my own work. I didn't use 'Ghost writers' because they do get ink all over the sheets. Not only that, but they have a tendency to rephrase expressions into words that could not possibly emanate from the mouths of the so-called authors. I once read a book, supposedly written by a Champion golfer, in which he is alleged to have said, 'The hands supinate and pronate in turn, as the centrifugal force engendered by the pelvis pours power into the shot.' Now I have walked quite a few rounds with this golfer, and the only time I heard him speak was when his opponent's ball was sliced into the trees and he said, ' 'Ard luck, mate.' So I decided to go it alone, and put down my thoughts just as they came into my mind and I believe you'll get the message. Please forgive me if I doesn't speak as good English as what you does. It's really my own fault. If I had spent as much time in reading Philosophy as I have on the golf course trying to cure a built-in hook, I'd be 'plus-four' at Oxford!

TED RAY

INTRODUCTION

by

DAI REES, C.B.E.

It was in Llandudno that I first met Ted Ray on a golf course. My friend Ken Bousfield had been sitting at the same table during breakfast and had finally succumbed to the fervent plea that Ken should take him along to join us in a 'warming-up' round for the Penfold Tournament.

The first hole at the Maesdu Golf Course is a short one, and needs only a lofted iron. We drove off and Ken and I were safely on the green. Ted took a four wood and addressed the ball. As long as I live I shall never forget that swing. Believe me, I've tried, but I shall never forget it. The 'Swing'—if you'll pardon the expression—was not exactly in the groove, in fact it described a path that used to be known as 'Aeroplane Skywriting'.

It must be admitted, however, that by some miracle the club made contact, and in fact, when the ball came to rest it was actually nearer the hole than Ken's or mine. Not on the same green, of course, but one can't have everything. It was a pleasant enough round, and occasionally we caught a glimpse of him tacking his way across the fairways like a lone round-the-world yachtsman, and it wasn't until we reached the fourteenth hole that we knew he carried a putter. I must admit that not once did he lose his temper, battling on and apparently getting masochistic pleasure from his efforts.

Ted represents the great majority of golfers who are the Life-Blood of the game. Despite the frustrations, they return to the scenes of their crimes, week after week, their heads 'bloody but unbowed', and that's what I kept on telling him. 'Look at the ball a little longer.' You may catch a glimpse of Ted at most of the big competitions, a dedicated follower of the tournaments and possessed of a loyalty that is hard to believe. He has given pleasure to millions on the Stage, on the Radio, and on Television, and once, on a TV show I gave him a lesson, and finally got him

11

to hit one straight, but I don't think that camera will ever be the same again.

More power to your elbow, Ted (don't lift it on the backswing), keep the gags rolling off the Assembly Line, and try to keep the ball in play.

Dai Reed.

1. IT'S ONLY A GAME

Golf is a fascinating game. It has taken me nearly forty years to discover that I can't play it! That isn't strictly true, because I was once on the green of a 595-yard hole in two, I once holed out my second shot on a hole measuring 350 yards, and on one never-to-be-forgotten occasion I holed my tee shot on a hole measuring 167 yards. But these were the happy moments of my golfing life. They are far outweighed by the sad times. Like taking a new ball out of the paper and slicing it out of bounds into corn that was even deeper than some of my jokes! But I hope you get my meaning.

My lowest ever handicap was seven. That's good, but not good enough. One aims for perfection and if I had my time over again, the first thing I would do would be to go to a professional and have lessons. Just as one should never attempt to teach one's wife how to drive a car, one should never ask some well-meaning fellow-golfer to shown one the rudiments of the game. I know, and I will tell you.

Bert Rogers was a 'juvenile'—lead in a touring revue. He could sing in tune and he wore plus-fours. This combination was to me the absolute epitome of a touring 'pro'. Having entered Show Business almost purely for the purpose of lying in bed until noon, I quickly found that even this had its limitations, and a natural curiosity to find out what was going on in the world outside eventually got me out of bed at eight o'clock in the morning. I would wander down to the theatre and wait for the mail or watch the acrobats trying out new tricks and, during a week in Huddersfield, Bert Rogers came out through the stage door as I was going in, carrying a slender golf bag over his shoulder. When I asked him where he was going, he told me that there was a fellow at the opposition music hall who played golf, and they were to meet for a game. I asked him if I could come along and he said I could.

I must confess that I laughed when I saw them trying to hit the ball straight, and after three or four holes Bert looked at me and said, 'I suppose you think that this is easy?' and I said, 'Well yes, I think it is.' 'Right,' said Bert. 'Try it.' He handed me a club and then said, 'Now wait a moment. Let me show you what you have to do.' He then put a ball on to a little wooden peg and swung the club. The ball disappeared straight up his left trouser leg. This put my golfing career back about six years, because that is what I thought one had to do. It was three months before I managed it, and even then it was bloody painful. But the point was that I had become another victim of the Royal and Ancient game.

Since those early days I have played golf on over three hundred courses and in all sorts of conditions. Talk about being keen! I played in Durban when the weather was so hot that there were flies on the coloured caddie-boy's eyelids and he was too tired to brush them off. I have played in a wind that was so strong that I hit a straight drive and played my second shot from twenty yards *behind* the tee, and once at Hallamshire in Sheffield it rained so hard that it took me fifteen minutes to take off my wet clothes.

The strange thing is that if I had my time over, I would do it all again. That, my friends, is dedication. Let the Powers, that cancel horse-racing because the ground is too hard, that take the cosseted soccer players off the playing pitch because the ground is too soft, abandon a cricket match because of bad light, note that, while all this is going on, and worse, somewhere a muffled and mackintosh-swathed 'knocker' is walking around in deep rough muttering, 'It must be farther than this.'

There is an old Scot at my club. He is now a 'five-day member' and has a 'Hate-in' with another octogenarian every morning from Monday to Saturday. Pity they can't find a third . . . they would rival the famous THREE OLD LADIES! They cannot stand each other, these two old men. They wouldn't give each other a two-inch putt even if there was a Force 8 gale blowing behind the ball. When they enter the clubhouse at the ninth hole for coffee and one says, 'It's your turn to pay,' the other's hearing-aid falls out halfway through the sentence. I've seen him greasing his ear-plug in the locker-room. But they are stuck with each other. Isn't it wonderful? It's the only competitive spirit left for them. I know I shall shed a tear when one of them passes on. What will be left for the one remaining? Happily he doesn't think about it. I know I am right, because I saw one of them the other morning,

14

actually *practising*, half an hour before his opponent put in an appearance. I watched the tortured knotted backswing and saw him half-top the ball just past the ladies' tee. 'That's great, Freddie,' I shouted . . . 'Yes,' he replied. 'Wait till that bloody Scotsman turns up . . . I'VE GOT IT NOW!'

2. ON REDUCING ONE'S HANDICAP

The first thing I noticed on arriving in Northampton was a huge poster, across the top of which was printed in huge blue lettering, 'Jack Jackson and his Band'. My own name was somewhere in the middle with the usual assortment of jugglers and sea-lions. Jackson had formerly been lead trumpet with the great Jack Hylton combination and had then gone out with his own formation.

Up to the time of which I am writing, our paths had never crossed, and I wondered what sort of fellow he was. I didn't see him at rehearsal, but after the first house on the Monday night I went to his dressing-room and knocked on the door. He opened it and asked me in, and I saw a handsome man with blue eyes and a splendid physique. He was much taller than I, but this didn't worry me because nearly everybody is! I introduced myself and we chatted away and suddenly I noticed a bag of golf clubs in the corner of the room and I said, 'You play golf, then?' and Jackson nodded. 'What's your handicap?' I asked. 'I'm scratch,' replied Jackson. Automatically I stood up. It isn't often one is in the presence of a scratch man and this was a moment to be revered and savoured.

'I don't suppose you would be interested in playing a round with me?' I ventured. His handsome face creased into a smile. 'Why not?' he said. 'Be at the stage door tomorrow morning and I'll run you to the course in the Rolls.'

I walked out in a daze. A scratch man with a Rolls! No wonder I had little sleep that night. Tuesday dawned bright and clear, and at 8.30 am we were rolling along to the golf course and on arrival we were delighted to note that we appeared to be the first pair out. We went through the usual procedure and signed our names in the book and changed our shoes and made our way to the first tee. I didn't presume to ask Jackson if he wanted a small wager on the game, but to my surprise he said, 'Shall we have a little interest . . . say five bob?' I agreed.

My handicap was seventeen at the time so he had to give me the generous allowance of thirteen shots, and he said, 'OK, away you go, I'll let you have the honour.' I remember thinking to myself, 'I suppose this is the last time I'll have it,' and I swung nice and easily and my ball sailed straight down the fairway. 'Very good,' said Jackson in appreciation, and he teed up a brand-new ball straight out of the wrapper. He took a full and very fast backswing and the ball soared away to the right and disappeared for ever over the railway lines. This was a slice. Believe me, I

Automatically I stood up . . .

know a slice when I see one, but I had never seen one like *that* before. I didn't have to wait long to see another because two new balls in rapid succession followed. I could hardly believe my eyes.

Jackson was completely unruffled. 'Strange,' he murmured. 'I don't usually slice the ball.' Out came another new ball. I had to say something. 'Please,' I implored, 'put down an old one.' 'Sorry,' smiled Jackson, 'I've never *had* an old one.' He swung again. This time the ball went perfectly straight. Unfortunately it hardly became airborne. We found it in the rough, about thirty yards in front of the tee.

By the time I played my second shot, I had practically forgotten all I'd ever learned about the game. I managed to scramble a five. Jackson holed out in thirteen. 'That puts you one up,' he said. 'Yes,' I replied, 'I know.' I always was very good at mathematics. That day I had to be. When we finished, and I had won by a mile, we adjourned to the bar. I turned to Jackson and said, 'Do you know what your score was?' 'No, I don't,' he replied. I told him. 'You took one hundred and eight.' 'Yes,' he said. 'I had an off day.' I was silent for a moment and then I said 'And what did you say your handicap was?' 'Scratch,' he said, looking me straight in the eye.

The following week I noticed that Jack Jackson and his Band were appearing at the Finsbury Park Empire. Also on the bill, giving a demonstration, was Henry Cotton. I sent Jackson a telegram. It simply said, 'Try to get a game with Cotton . . . he's scratch too!'

Some ten years ago Jack Jackson sold his home here and migrated to sunny Puerto de la Cruz in Tenerife, in the Canary Isles. A couple of years ago I went there for a holiday, and I went to the sporting golf course in the centre of the island to see if I could find him. It was a lovely day, but there were few people about at lunchtime, in fact the only person I could see was a tiny Spanish boy with the largest brown eyes I have ever seen. 'Are you a caddie?' I inquired. '*Si*, señor,' he answered. 'Do you know Mr Jack Jackson?' I went on. '*Si*', replied the little boy. 'I often carry hees clubs.' 'I don't suppose you know his handicap do you?' I asked. '*Si*,' he said, grinning. 'Señor Jackson is scratch.'

My own personal handicap as I have said has never been lower than seven, although on inspired occasions I have played to less. Which reminds me of an occasion some years ago when I was doing a week at the Winter Gardens theatre in Margate. I had been a great success and on the Saturday night at the end of my act I had taken six curtains. Unfortunately the manager saw me do it and I had to put them back. That's a joke and I'm glad I got it out of my system!

After the show I somehow became involved with some people and, although still a little hazy as to how it all happened, I ended up in someone's house at a party. It was a hectic affair and some time in the early hours I passed out. When I awoke I looked around and the first person I saw was Larry Gains, the famous Canadian heavyweight boxer. 'Where are we?' I said. 'I don't know,' replied Larry. I looked at my watch. It was a quarter to six in the morning. I shot up. 'Good Heavens!' I gasped. 'I have to be on the first tee at Crews Hill at eight forty-five!'

I felt like death, but a golf date is a golf date and I ran to the station and collapsed into a carriage. I arrived at the golf course at 8.40 am and the three chaps who made up the Sunday morning four-ball were annoyed. 'Come on!' they yelled. 'What time do you call this?'

I could understand their annoyance. The four waiting to go off behind us were the slowest lot in the club and I knew that if they went off before we did, it would mean 'Goodbye drinking time' and a late lunch.

'Just change my shoes,' I shouted, and I dashed into the locker-room. I put my hand into my pocket. No keys and the clubs were in the locker. I was desperate. Suddenly I had a thought. Borrow some clubs. I looked for an open locker and found one, and the name on the door said 'Roy Peskett'. Roy is a Fleet Street journalist and a good friend. He didn't come to the club much so I thought I'd be safe in borrowing his clubs and I knew he wouldn't mind.

I pulled open the door and there was his bag. The wooden clubs seemed to have transparent head covers, but on closer inspection these proved to be spider's webs—as I've said Roy didn't play very often! I dragged them out and examined them. They weren't exactly a matched set. In fact, the collection consisted of an old-fashioned 'baffy' with a rounded sole, an ancient cleek, four mashie-niblicks, and a putter with a leaden head.

I reached the first tee and I had a splitting headache. 'We've already driven off,' said Johnny Burchall. I teed up and I was so tired that the club felt like a shovel. The ball went as straight as a die for at least 220 yards. I won't bore you with the whole card, but my gross score with all putts in was seventy-two. The par of the course was seventy-two. I had never done it in my life before and I have no reason to suppose that I shall do it again. I leaned on the bar at the nineteenth and downed my pint and the world had suddenly become a wonderful place. I have never been 'King for a day', but on one heavenly never-to-be-forgotten morning at the Crews Hill Golf Club, I was 'Scratch'.

19

3. CLOBBER

Fashion changes us. We don't seem to have much say in the matter. One day you are 'with it'. The next day you are without it. If you don't believe me, just take a look at some of those old golf books in your library that you haven't opened for some time. Trilby hats and Norfolk jackets. How did they ever play in garb like that? And, surprisingly, get around the course in 'level fours'. We just merge from one set of clothes into another without really noticing it.

Perhaps the most significant change in golfing attire has been in the way the women dress. 'Slacks', which are very often 'tights', have made their mark in no uncertain fashion. Just the other day a friend and I were following a lady in a pair of trousers that were crying for mercy. 'Ted,' mused my friend, 'it looks like two kids fighting under a blanket.' After all there are very few women who can wear slacks and get away with it, and still look feminine.

I'm not trying to be unkind. I love women. I should! After all, if my mother hadn't been one, I wouldn't be here! But, girls, please! Those so-called 'Bermuda' shorts. They come to just below the knee, and, one supposes, prevent bee- and wasp-stings. But why 'Bermuda'? Are the sting-equipped insect-attackers only indigenous to Bermuda? Do they not foregather and get into mass-formation in Cannes, Cairo, and Cleethorpes?

Me, I like to see a woman dressed in a skirt. There is nothing more beautiful than to see her turn her waist and swish her hips and send the ball soaring down the fairway. The memorable 'Babe' Zaharias, when asked the secret of her long and beautiful driving from the tee, remarked, 'I just hitch up my girdle and whack the hell out of the ball.' Bless her! She could put her drive well past that of many men and still look feminine.

But enough of the women (as Henry VIII might have said when he threw his last chicken leg over his shoulder). How about Homo Sapiens? (Homo = male, and sapiens . . . just a sap when trying to find an excuse for late arrival home after the Saturday morning four-ball!) What about *their* 'clobber'? My wife com-

20

plains at golf-club dinner-dances when she sees mud on the turn-ups of my dress-suit. 'Turn-ups?' I know I'm not 'with-it' but is it *my* fault that I've been doing so well in knock-out competitions that sometimes I have to go straight from the course to the ballroom? Good Heavens, I haven't seen my tailor for years. I should think he's dead and gone by now, anyway. He really wasn't much of a tailor. Fancy making me a set of 'plus-twos' with only one leg? I still think that I only got them because Long John Silver didn't turn up for a second fitting.

But at least I *do* try to look presentable on the course. After all, to paraphrase Walter Hagen, you don't have to be a golfer, but at least you can *look* like one. I know many who don't. The same old green-looking pullover that once was blue, the pants that look like they've been worn out from the *inside*, and the inevitable rubber waterproof shoewear that *isn't*. WHY? I suppose the wearers would feel uncomfortable in any other garb, and can you blame 'em? I'm speaking specifically of the *senior* members of the club. Dress them in cashmere twin-sets, give them lustrous 'with-it' trousers with fifteen-inch bottoms, co-respondents' shoes in black-and-white and a jockey cap that looks like a Lester Piggott reject, and do you mean to tell me that they would be happy? I've news for you . . . they wouldn't even get off the first tee.

It's all right for the younger brigade, of course. They were born into it and it makes them feel like affluent young 'pros'. Good luck to them. And as far as I am concerned they can have it.

No, sir, the correct outfit for the middle-to-ageing golfers is a nice Jaeger shirt worn with the club tie. A warm pullover into which he can change at the course in a matter of seconds. A pair of flannel trousers that can be turned up twice in the winter months, and wide enough to slip over his shoes, and a pair of stout rubbers that will keep his feet dry. He can keep the latter under his locker until they change the locker-room attendant, or until the club burns down. There's only one snag with this outfit. You will be changed for going home so rapidly that it will always be you who buys the first drink. And why not? It's only a game, and the company of fellow-golfers is a wonderful part of one's life. 'Oh *no*. You don't mean to tell me that it's raining? Pass my cycle clips—I don't want my socks to get wet!'

4. THE PERFECT SHOT

The nicest description of golf I ever read stated that 'Golf is a game where a man places a small sphere on top of a larger sphere and attempts to dislodge the small sphere from the larger sphere'.

Well, a golf ball and the world have this in common, that they are both round. Of course sometimes the small object gets badly knocked about, but what about the larger sphere? Some nations do all they can to try to bash it out of all recognition.

Of course the object of the game of golf is to propel the ball forward on a straight line towards the hole. When the ball enters the hole in one stroke, perfection has been achieved. Well, nearly. One of our old members trundled a spoon shot forward one Sunday morning and half-topped the shot. The ground was bone-hard and the ball rolled forward some 160 yards, disappeared into a dried river bed, climbed up the other side, and ran forward into the hole! I noticed that whenever one brought up the story of his hole-in-one, he quickly changed the subject. I should think so too. Fate is very capricious in its distribution of 'holes-in-one'. Some of the greatest professional golfers in the world have never achieved it, and yet the late and beautiful Gertrude Lawrence accomplished it with the very first shot she ever played. What an anticlimax the game must have seemed after that!

At Meyrick Park, Bournemouth, a gentleman named Morton did the same hole-in-one stroke *twice in the same day*. Talk about the Treble Chance or Ernie's £50,000 Premium Bond Prize, but what are the odds against Mr Morton's feat? Incalculable I should think.

One morning, playing in a three-ball at Highgate, the secretary told us that the first short hole on the course had been altered and a new green laid. 'You will be the first golfers ever to play the new hole,' he informed us.

Out we went, my brother-in-law George, his friend Tommie Morris, and yours truly. Tommie won't mind my saying that the standard of his golf was such that he considered himself lucky to hit the wall of a barn from the inside! We came to the short hole. Tommie teed up. 'This is a new green, Tom,' I remarked. 'Don't damage it.' 'I won't,' said Tommie. Yes, you've guessed it, he holed in one.

The famous bandleader Henry Hall was out practising one day when he heard a voice from the roadside hedge. 'No, no, for heaven's sake!' barked the voice. Henry looked up to see a gentleman in hunting pink mounted on a magnificent hunter. 'Let me show you, you're doing it all wrong.' Henry meekly handed

There. That's the way . . .

over the club, and the sportsman addressed a ball and gave the club a vigorous swish. The ball flew as straight as a die and ended in the hole. 'There,' said the stranger. 'That's the way,' and he mounted his horse and disappeared from Henry's sight for ever.

I played with a comedian named Howard Rogers in a competition some years ago. Howard was very funny. On the stage intentionally but on the golf course, not at all.

He was a 'stage' parson and his sermon to his imaginary

audience really was a classic. 'One of the dairymaids has been disqualified from next week's milking competition,' he said. 'Last week she was caught practising with a pound of sausages under the kitchen table.' 'That was funny,' I told him, but believe me it wasn't half as funny as Howard's backswing. Firstly he would expel all the air from his lungs, then slowly take the club back round, then up, forward and back again, and lash at the ball so vigorously that he pirouetted on his left toe and finished with his back to the hole. Even Gary Player would have found it difficult to make contact with a swing like that, but Howard managed it somehow, and he wasn't wearing his parson's make-up either! Those celluloid collars can be very sharp!

I liked old Howard very much and I was pleased to mark his card, but at the same time I was glad that I had paid attention to my Maths teacher at school. It was a lovely sunny day at Sudbury and we arrived eventually at the sixteenth hole. It's a short hole and the tee is way up above the green so that even if you half-top the ball it will run downhill. It was one of those summer days when the ground is baked as hard as a traffic-warden's heart, but to my amazement Howard proceeded to take the two wood out of his bag. 'What *are* you doing?' I asked him in astonishment, 'That's *far* too much club.' He looked at me benignly over his spectacles. 'Very unorthodox,' he answered, 'but very effective.' He then concentrated on that terrible backswing and hit the ball straight towards the hole. It bounced once and shot right into the cup. I suppose I should have known it would happen. Parsons never lie. You have never seen a happier man walk into the bar. Again and again he recounted the story and at last he said, 'Of course, my dear friend Ray thought I was mad, but it proved I knew what I was about.' 'Yes,' I said, 'but you didn't tell them what your score was on the fifteenth and seventeenth holes. Seven, and an eight. I don't want to spoil your day, but if it hadn't been for your hole in one at the sixteenth, for those three holes you'd have been level fives.'

On 28 May I was playing at Crews Hill, my home course, and halfway round it began to rain. I was playing with newly acquired clubs and not doing very well with them, and on the twelfth hole I was in two ditches and was rapidly losing my temper. We came to the thirteenth tee and I took out my Number 2 iron and teed up a new ball. I thought, 'I'll just take an easy swing and let the club do the work.' The ball flew straight and true and hit the green, bounced once, and then seemed to become jammed between the flagstick and the edge of the hole.

My companions said, 'It looks like it's in!' and my caddie, a gangling youth of fifteen, tore off for the green like a hare. I ran after him shouting, 'Leave it alone,' because I sensed that he was running to take out the flagstick and might easily have wrenched the ball out too. If he had, I think I would have belted him with a five iron, and no golf-minded jury would have been able to con-

Leave it alone!

vict me. Mercifully when he was some ten yards from the hole, the ball disappeared.

I've been very close to doing another hole in one on many occasions, but have never quite succeeded. A little while ago, on a bright and sunny day, I took my paintbox to the thirteenth hole at Crews Hill and painted a reasonable canvas of 'my' hole and presented it to the Club. They graciously accepted it and it hangs on the wall of the card-room.

I stood there looking at it the other day, and Big Henry Crick came in. 'It's not bad,' he said, 'but you have left out one thing.' I looked puzzled. 'What's that?' I asked. '*My* ball,' said Henry. 'It's always in that big cross-bunker in front of the green.'

5. THE ACHILLES HEEL—OR TOE!

A three-handicap golfer of my acquaintance teed up at the first hole of the Old Course at St Andrews, and asked his caddie for a three iron. The old Scotsman's jaw dropped and so did the golf bag. 'What's the matter?' asked my friend in surprise. 'Wha's the matter?' replied the caddie heatedly . . . 'Ye're takin' an iron on the first tee at St Andraes? . . . Ye'll caddie for yo're ruddy sel'.'

You must admit that it does seem like sacrilege, but there *were* extenuating circumstances. John had recently been hitting everything off the toe with his woods. You'll be glad to know that he has now solved the problem. He's had half the clubhead cut off and he uses the larger ball. He no longer hits them off the toe. He misses the ball altogether and the only games he gets are with new members!

I think that the average handicap golfer has at least one club in his bag of which he is afraid. This does no great harm, unless it is the putter, in which case he might as well stay in the club lounge and play chess. Putting is a game within a game, and some of the greatest non-winners of Championships failed tragically when it came to the simple task of tapping a ball some four feet, or less, into the hole. Drives from the tee a mile long, iron shots rifled deep to the heart of the green, but when it came to the simple putt, some of these men took on the appearance of petrified trees. They almost appeared to take root, and just could not get the club started back from the ball.

Barry Piddock, on the other hand, was one of the world's great putters. 'Who is Barry Piddock?' I hear you ask. Let me tell you. He was the manager of a touring show in which I was the leading comedian. Our Sundays were spent journeying from town to town (usually with a wait at Crewe) and it made one feel pretty depressed.

One Saturday evening, Barry came into my dressing-room. 'I shan't be with you on the train tomorrow,' he said. 'I'm travelling by car and my brother is taking me to Leamington to play golf against two members there.' 'Lucky devil,' I said as I thought of the flat beer and the sausage rolls at Crewe.

The following Monday morning I was taking my band call at the Hippodrome, Birmingham, and Barry walked in. He was beaming. 'All right, Bighead,' I joked. 'Tell me what happened.' He told me. He had *one-putted eighteen greens*! As you can imagine, this news knocked me sideways. I pumped his arm. 'Fabulous! Fantastic!' I shouted. 'What did you win by?' 'Win?' said Barry. 'We lost the match *and* the Bye.' Barry was nothing if not truthful and I believed him, because the fact is that although he was the greatest putter I ever saw, the rest of his game was not memorable. He didn't care though. Those eighteen single putts had made the world look rosy. His gross score was ninety-eight and it was the first time he had ever broken 100!

Ben Hogan has said that his favourite club is the Number 5 iron. It seems to him that this is the 'middle' club and he likes it. Then why not a bagful of '5-irons'? It might save a lot of grief. Of course there is a restriction on the number of clubs we are allowed to have in the golf bag. The number is fourteen, and I have been told that the committee of the Royal and Ancient is the body responsible for this decision. I reckon that they are all caddies and are worried about the weight, otherwise why should they put up this ban at all? If they wanted to do the average golfer a bit of good, they should restrict the number to nine and cut out almost half of the misery.

After all, Young Tom Morris and Old Tom Morris and the top-notch golfers of their day went round with eight clubs and a gutty ball and completed the round in level fours! How do you fancy YOUR chances of doing that with a set of swing-weight-balanced clubs, and remember that in those days they didn't have fine-edged blades on a motor-mower to manicure the greens. The greenkeepers then were sheep, which was all right if you could avoid the droppings. No wonder they abolished the 'Stymie' rule!

I know a man who has a set of fourteen clubs and they are all made of wood, including the putter. Claims he's afraid of being struck by lightning. You can't really blame him when you remember that Johnny White, the slender, talented inside forward of the Tottenham Hotspur Football Club was out having a lonely 'knock' at the Crews Hill Golf Club in Enfield when a storm blew up, a storm that brought thunder and a fork of lightning. Lightning that ripped the umbrella out of the hand of

27

my fellow-club member Alex Paterson and tore across the course to end the life of John White as he took shelter under a tree.

I play almost every Sunday morning with a southpaw named Norman Fish. Norman has heard all the jokes about his name . . . 'Left-handed Fish', 'Fish and Chip shots', 'Fish has taken a battering', and when someone has holed a twelve-yard putt, 'All right, Fish, take the bones out of that,' and Norman just smiles and nods. 'How true, how true,' he says, sadly.

Norman has a beautiful set of clubs, no codding. (Sorry!) Strangely though, he can't play the six iron. There's something funny about it, especially when *he's* using it. 'Look,' he once remarked to me, 'the loft on it is just the same as the loft on your nine iron.' He took the nine iron out of my bag and laid the clubs side by side. 'See what I mean?' he inquired. 'Yes, I do,' I replied. I lied, of course, and it didn't prove anything. So why does he bother? More of that later. Wasn't there a famous US professional who had a favourite driver? 'Couldn't play without it,' he would tell you. It gave him confidence even though the club had had five new heads and six new shafts!

I must confess that my own Achilles heel has nothing to do with the clubs. It's that little pitch and run from twenty-five to thirty yards from the flag. My three companions on Sunday morning all play it with ease. Big Henry Crick can do it with his eyes shut. Jack Stone shuts the face of the club and lays them dead. Norman Fish plays the shot better than many pros. (Not with a six iron, of course!) Kids can do it, grey-haired ladies adore it, so why should I have been sorted out to fluff it? I once spent three days at Selsdon Park with Harry Weetman and he finally got me to get the feel of the shot and to my delight I was chipping them up to the pin like clockwork. I slept well that night and next morning I was loading my things into the car when I thought, 'I'll just go out and try a dozen before I go home.' I missed the first one altogether, topped the next three, and left. Of course everyone has given me advice. 'Forget the right hand, pull it through with the left.' 'Cut off your left hand, just push it through with the right.' 'Play it like you would a putt.'

Nothing works for me. I hit two good woods on a hole measuring 496 yards. There I am some thirty yards from the green. What do I do as I walk to my ball? I whistle. I think of the lovely lunch Sybil is preparing for me. I think of the time I almost 'stopped the show' at a Command Performance at the London Palladium.

Finally I have to play the shot, and I take a club from my bag. Which one? Decisions, decisions. The wedge, the four iron, or maybe the four wood. What am I talking about? Sanity returns. Take the Number 8, it's a nice safe club. Practice swing. Lovely. Address the ball. I can feel three pairs of eyes boring into the back of my neck. They know as well as I, that I am going to make a mess of it. Oh no I'm not! Positive thinking, that's it. You can do it, son. Head still, and slowly back. Oh yes? How much punishment can a man take? Suddenly it's all over, quick snatch back down into the turf and half a divot, just like a trap door, and easy to replace. 'Good morning, worms.' Pick up ball, fake smile. 'I'll leave it to you, partner,' and walk to the next tee to wait for the other three. 'I'll give the game up,' I mutter to myself, knowing that I never will.

I've often thought that I could devise a special club to get all this out of my system. Quite illegal, of course, but very effective. I'm going to call it 'The Concave Scrambler' and the blade will be perfectly straight except for a recess in the centre something like an egg cup. I shall take a very short backswing, then bring down the face of the club where the ball will be received by the hollowed-out face and *lifted* on to the green. It will be marketed secretly of course, and sold strictly under the counter, so please order early as I am sure that there will be a fantastic demand. It must never be used in competitions of course.

Once again I ask, 'Why do we use so many clubs?' How long is it since you saw anyone (professionals always excepted of course) use a two wood on the fairway? They fluff it and say, 'I should have had a spoon.' So take the three wood. Mind you the number *four* wood has a little more comforting loft and with the average golfer is only some ten yards shorter for length than the three wood. So forget the three wood, and we have rid ourselves of two clubs already! The four wood is as good as, and safer than the three iron, so forget the three iron. Your four iron is a nice club, retain it and keep your five iron (Ben Hogan), throw away the six iron (Norman Fish), seven is a lucky number, so that one stays in the bag. The nine iron will get you into, and out of, just as many bunkers as the wedge and sand iron put together. Buy a 'Concave Scrambler' (order early) and your favourite putter, and you have eight clubs which you can easily carry in a 'drain-pipe' golfbag.

Hey, wait a minute, I've just had a thought. What about that thirty yards pitch and run that gives me so much trouble? I could hit it along the ground with a drainpipe bag! Well no, I don't think *anyone* would stand for that!

6. A STRANGE HAPPENING

Four of us were in the bar one Sunday morning. Our four-ball is always the first to finish, although we don't reach the nineteenth as quickly as we used to because the game has become so popular and we have admitted so many new members. So it was actually on the seventeenth green last Remembrance Sunday at 11 am, where we paused while the guns reverberated, out of respect for golfers and non-golfers alike, all long gone.

'I shan't be with you next Sunday, lads,' I remarked as we downed our first half-pint of the day (just to settle the dust, as big Henry says). 'I'm going away for my twenty-fifth Wedding Anniversary.' 'Where are you going?' asked Jack. (He's a bachelor, but he's not lonely, if you get my point.) 'Well, actually,' I said casually, 'we're off to Gleneagles.' 'Who, you and the wife?' inquired Norman. 'Don't be silly,' I said. 'Me and the caddie!' Well, I have to have my little joke. Jack looked at me. 'How on earth did you get your wife to agree to Gleneagles?'

'Well, you won't believe it, but it was her idea,' I answered.

Of course they didn't believe me, but nevertheless it was true. Sybil adores the game, although she doesn't play. Every year I take her to a couple of the big tournaments and we walk around and follow the play and lunch in the big marquee. It was at Wentworth that we sat at the same table as two dear old gentlemen and I could see by their eyes that they had recognized me. They were much too polite to say so but, when I had gone for the coffee, one of them remarked to Sybil, 'May we say that your husband has given us so much pleasure?' 'Thank you,' she replied. 'Me too!'

So off we went to Scotland and stayed at the famous Gleneagles Hotel, where I met a very charming Scot and we played both the King's Course and the Queen's in one day.

In that lovely part of the world it doesn't get dark until very late, and after dinner my wife looked out of the window and said, 'You have a drink with the boys in the bar, dear, and I think I'll walk round the King's Course again.' Word of Honour that is true. Imagine fifty-four holes without hitting a shot; the way I've been performing lately I think I'll join her.

Most married men experience only *one* Silver Wedding and those in Show Business don't advertise it much, possibly because it gives away their age in a world that is becoming increasingly the scene of the younger man. Another reason is that some of us try to keep away from the limelight when we are not being paid for being in the public eye. It was for this reason that I insisted on registering in the hotel in my own name, and not that of my stage pseudonym. Sybil was disappointed. She wanted to tell the whole world that we had experienced twenty-five years of happy marriage, but I was adamant.

However, I had miscalculated the perspicacity and resource of the management. When the telegrams began to arrive they had put two and twenty-five together and, as we walked into the dining-room, the head waiter conducted us to our table whereon was a cake with twenty-five candles lit. A charming couple from Edinburgh were at the next table, and Mrs Lumley produced a beautiful bouquet of red roses and, as she handed them to my missus, the band struck up 'The Anniversary Waltz'. We looked at each other, but I couldn't see her very clearly, because my eyes weren't focusing properly.

The next day Mr and Mrs Lumley had gone back to Edinburgh and I was without a golfing partner, so I went over to the Caddie-master and asked him if he could find me someone around middle handicap who would like a game. 'Oh, ye're playing in the Silver Tassie, are ye?' he grinned. 'Now come on, Jock,' I laughed. 'You know I'm not nearly good enough for that.' The Silver Tassie Competition brings together some of the finest amateurs in Scotland, and the winning score would almost certainly be among the first twenty in the 'OPEN'. 'I'm sorry, sir,' said Jock, 'but both the King's Course and the Queen's will be in use for the competition for the next two days.' 'Then what am I to do?' I begged. 'Weel, sir,' advised Jock, 'We have a nice little nine-hole course here too, so why not go down there and you're almost certain to have it to yersel'.' 'Very well,' I vouchsafed. (I'm awfully sorry about that last word, but I've been dying to use it for years, and the opportunity doesn't often arise when you're doing a cabaret performance.)

Sybil had gone off somewhere ... she was either walking

round the King's Course or smelling the roses from the Lumleys, so I made my solitary way to the nine-hole course, which was, as the admirable Jock Crichton had stated, quite deserted. I teed up and was just about to drive off when I noticed a figure on a bicycle approaching along the road that leads to the hotel, and I paused for a moment in case my built-in slice reared its ugly head. To my surprise, the rider dismounted, and leaning the cycle against a tree, walked over towards me. 'Guid mornin',' he said in a lovely Scottish accent. 'Would ye' be lookin' for a game?' I stared at him, rather rudely I'm afraid, but he did present a rather unusual figure.

He was very slight, almost thin, and he carried on his shoulder a 'drainpipe' golf bag. It contained about six clubs, and *what clubs*! They appeared to have been borrowed from one of those golf museums. He must have thought me rather rude because it was a minute or so before I spoke. 'Yes, of course,' I said eventually, and he smiled his thanks. He motioned that I should take the honour, and I said, 'Would you like to have half a crown or a ball on the game, sir?' He shook his head. 'Oh no, thank you, I never play for money.' I took my shot, a pretty fair one for me, and the ball finished on the left-hand side of the fairway at a distance of some 200 yards. 'Good shot, sir!' exclaimed my opponent, and he teed up a ball.

What followed was, and still is, unbelievable. The thin man performed the most elegant golf swing I have ever seen, and I've seen most of them. The ball took off like the climb of a jet-plane, and landed plumb in the centre of the fairway, not fantastically long, but perfect. I won't bore you with the actual figures but at the end of that nine-hole round he had completed every hole in the exact par score. No birdies, no bogies, but strict perfection par.

Just before his departure he told me his name. David McIntosh. 'Thank ye verra much,' he smiled. 'I really enjoyed that game.' I wish I could have agreed. Although I liked his company very much, I hadn't won a single hole and halved only three. But it was a privilege to have seen him play. He slung the little bag over his shoulder, straddled his bike and rode off. I never saw him again.

The strange thing was, that a few years later I was sitting in the lounge of a Perth hotel. As I idly turned over the pages

Never saw him again . . .

of the local paper, an item caught my eye. It said, 'Among the items for sale yesterday were the unclaimed effects of the late David McIntosh, who lived alone and apparently had no relatives. The items consisted of a bicycle, a small golf bag, and a Bible.'

7. WHERE IT REALLY COUNTS

I have written in a previous chapter about the extraordinary performance of Barry Piddock and his eighteen single putts in one round. Barry's putting style was not remarkable; he just had an uncanny eye for the lines to the hole.

It is very strange to see how some of the great golfers with perfect swings change in their attitudes when it comes to getting the ball into the hole on the green. All the grace and rhythm seem to go. They appear to be like praying mantisses or appealing clergymen, or even acrobats attempting to do the splits in the effort to cajole that small pill to drop.

Once at the Mere Country Club I suddenly realized that I was being watched by the great Scottish pro George Duncan, and I slid the ball past the rim of the hole. 'Oh, George,' I said lamely, 'I should have taken more time over that putt.' 'Nonsense,' replied George. 'Walk up to it and get it over with . . . you haven't got *time* to make a mistake.' And there's something in that. I have played with chaps who stared at the ball so long, that one was almost forced to scream, 'For God's sake *hit it!*'

I am sure that some golfers do this deliberately, for nowhere else in this game of golf is there more gamesmanship indulged in than there is on the putting green. One 'sportsman' of my acquaintance, standing just close enough for one to see his feet, would slowly—oh ever so slowly—cross his feet just as one took the putter back from the ball. After three holes you were waiting for it!

Another would knock your ball two feet away from the hole when it didn't matter, but later in the round, when it did, would ask you to sink a fifteen-inch putt. Of course you invariably missed it!

'Old Yorky', a golf bag 'humper' who came from Yorkshire (hence his nickname) and occasionally carried for me when P.R.O. jobs were scarce once said, 'D'ye know Mr Ray, there's only two kinds of bloody fools at golf, them as gives putts and them as won't tak' em.' It is sad to see a truly great player get that dreaded disease known as 'the yips'. The sweet swing is still

35

there but once on the green, the rot sets in. Dear old Charlie Whitcombe once told me, 'Ted, I would have won the OPEN, if only I could have holed the "tiddlers". There were times when I couldn't get the putter back on a three-foot putt to save my life and I've had to walk away from the ball and start all over again!' It's readily understandable when you realize that a final putt of four feet for a title today can be worth £200 per inch!

It was surely one of the longest putts in history that won our Ladies' Club handicap for Mrs Ogilvy. Her opponent in the final was a smashing bird named Barbara Trevelyen who really was by far the superior golfer. Lady Luck was certainly 'caddying' for Mrs Ogilvy that day, and poor Barbara was having none at all. In fact as they stood on the eighteenth tee the match was all square. Barbara smashed her ball some 220 yards down the fairway and the ball must have landed in a small hole or rabbit scrape, because it took a vicious kick to the right and shot into a bunker. Mrs Ogilvy heaved her considerable girth and hooked her tee shot to the left and it actually struck the 'out of bounds' notice board, and bounced back on to the fairway! She half-topped her second which trundled on and on along the hard ground and her ball finished some twenty yards short of the green. Her opponent played a really beautiful recovery shot, and the ball landed on the green about five yards away from the flag. The elderly lady then took out her putter and was obviously playing for safety. Then she putted. And what a putt! From the moment she struck the ball, I knew it would finish near the hole. On and on it ran as if drawn by a magnet. It rattled against the stick and dropped in!

Barbara's face was a study. How *could* anyone be so lucky? She lined up her putt carefully and the ball just edged the hole and stopped some three inches away. Mrs Ogilvy was delighted and moved forward to shake hands with her opponent. Their finger-tips barely met and the younger woman muttered something under her breath and walked away quickly to the clubhouse. Mrs Ogilvy was near to tears and, ignoring the congratulations of her friends, she made her way to the secretary's office. As she entered he looked up and could see at once that the old lady was upset. 'Whatever is the matter?' he inquired. 'It's that young Miss Trevelyen,' bleated Mrs Ogilvy. 'I have just beaten her in the Club Handicap and just because I sank a long putt I heard her call me a "lucky old cow".' The secretary arose and put a comforting arm around her shoulder. 'Now, my dear,' he consoled, 'I shouldn't worry about that. I've been secretary here for thirty years and they *still* call me "Major". We're all vulnerable I suppose.'

It is said that the great J. H. Taylor had a short putt to tie for a championship and, missing it, was so incensed that he hurled the offending putter high over the heads of the crowd, where it was retrieved by a small boy. A spectator grabbed him by the arm and demanded that he hand over the putter. 'No,' said the lad firmly. 'He threw it away and it's mine!' 'Look,' said the man, 'I'll give

Hurled the offending putter . . .

you a shilling for it.' Well, a shilling being what it was in those days, the boy accepted the offer. Years later the man was playing at Westward Ho! and, as he was approaching the eighteenth green, his opponent said, 'Do you know that the gentleman sitting in that chair in front of the clubhouse is the great J. H. Taylor?' 'Why, what a remarkable thing,' replied the other, 'I've got his putter in my bag!'

He then recounted the story of how he had acquired the club from the small boy. 'Wait a minute,' he exclaimed. 'Wouldn't it be a wonderful thing if I walked up to the Grand Old Man and presented him with his putter after all these years?' 'Marvellous!' replied his friend. 'What a splendid idea.' They completed the final hole and approached the old gentleman. 'Mr Taylor,' began the man. 'I have here the putter that you threw away many years ago when you failed to tie for the championship,' and he handed over the club to J.H. The Grand Old Man was touched and a tear came into his eye as he took the putter and gazed at it reflectively. It was a poignant moment and nobody spoke.

Then J. H. Taylor stood up. 'Aye,' he said. 'And you can keep the ruddy thing,' and for the second time in his life he hurled the club away, with all the strength that his arm could muster. Memory, like tradition, dies hard.

It was at the Keighley Golf Club in Yorkshire where I missed a short putt on the eighteenth (isn't it funny that all the drama seems to happen on the eighteenth—golfers hardly ever mention the long one that dropped at the first and which probably decided the game) and a nice Yorkshire gentleman stopped me on the way to the locker-room and said, 'You are not the first and most certainly you won't be the last to miss a putt like that,' and he proceeded to recount a remarkable story.

It appeared that a few years previously one of the members (he didn't give the name so we'll call him Joe Doakes) had 'yipped' the ball away from the hole at almost the identical spot from where I'd just played mine, and his opponent (let's call him Harry Bragg) had found it amusing. Angry words were exchanged, and finally Doakes said, 'I'll bet you twenty pounds that you won't get one in from the same distance.' 'Don't be an idiot,' sneered Bragg. 'I could do it all day with my eyes shut.' 'Wait a minute,' said Doakes. 'There is one stipulation, you must wait three months and do it at noon on May 1st.' Bragg shrugged his shoulders. 'Fine with me,' he laughed. 'The bet is on.'

The story-teller chuckled and continued. 'The news spread around the Club and some of the members even struck bets on the result. The weeks went by. Doakes seemed calm enough, and always appeared to be smiling, but Bragg, on the other hand, seemed rather worried and could often be seen behind the club-house on the practice green slotting two-foot putts one after the other. Eventually the dramatic day arrived, and about two hundred members were grouped around the eighteenth green as the two men emerged from the clubhouse. Joe Doakes was sucking his pipe contentedly, and Bragg was smiling bravely. The

Yorkshire gentleman paused. 'The tension was almost unbearable as our secretary appeared on the scene and with a tape measure peeled off exactly twenty-four inches. Bragg took out a brand-new ball and carefully placed it on the designated spot.' I could hardly wait to hear the end of the story. 'Well, go on,' I said. 'What happened?'

'Bragg was about to address the ball when Doakes spoke . . . "Just a moment, old man," he said. "Would you care to double the bet on condition that the forty pounds goes to Charity?" Bragg breathed heavily. "Done," he said, and as he placed the blade of his putter behind the ball, there was a silence that could actually be felt.' The old man paused. 'I know,' I cried. 'You're going to tell me that Bragg missed the putt!' 'More than that,' said the story-teller. 'He didn't even make contact with the ball, but hit the turf behind.' He smiled. 'Mind you, he got the next one in, but it's always easier when the pressure's off, don't you think?'

8. SYDNEY

If you attended 'Ladies' Night' at the Savoy, The Dorchester, The Grosvenor House, or indeed, at any of the larger London Hotels, during the period following the Second World War and into the Fifties, it is more or less certain that you danced to the music of Sydney Jerome and his Band.

Sydney seldom took off his evening dress clothes from October until the following March, for he was in great demand. He was of medium height with a red face and a chin that jutted out like the Rock of Gibraltar, and one might have been forgiven for thinking he was of a pugnacious nature had it not been for his twinkling blue eyes. He loved his golf and got down to a very genuine nine handicap, and the measure of his accuracy can be judged by the fact that on no less than five occasions he accomplished a hole-in-one. After the last of these he walked into the clubhouse and said to the assembled Sons-of-Suction, 'Anyone want to buy a putter?'

As my wife and I danced around the bandstand his face would break into a grin, and he would conduct the orchestra with the baton held in both hands with the overlapping grip showing three knuckles.

His work inevitably kept him out late at night, and on one occasion he arrived home at around 3 am and, as he let himself into the hall, he noticed his golf bag leaning against the umbrella stand. Taking a seven iron, he faced the large mirror on the wall and took a full practice swing. Unfortunately Syd's eyes were correctly glued to the carpet and the next second there came the terrible sound of shattered glass as the head of the club buried itself in the chandelier, and Sydney's bull-neck became studded with diamond-like slivers of glass.

The next minute a slender little lady appeared at the head of the staircase clad in a nightie and her hair in curlers. It was, of course, Cathie, Syd's wife. She gazed on the scene and then gave voice to what I think was a classic summation of the whole event. 'Oh, Sydney,' she cried . . . 'Now what have you done?'

Arthur Askey, for whom Sydney played the piano on many

occasions, said Syd was playing golf one day and drove his ball into deep rough. It was eventually found and Sydney took a lofted club and slashed at the ball with a vicious swing. To the amazement of all present, out came not one ball, but two. Jerome's caddie immediately fainted! Arthur ran across to the unfortunate caddie. 'What are you doing?' asked Syd. Arthur cried, 'I'm going to bring him to.' 'Great,' said Syd. 'Bring me one as well.' Happily the caddie recovered, and they all had one at the nineteenth.

In addition to his love of golf, Syd Jerome had a most unusual hobby. Trains. Not the usual electric or clockwork models, but the real thing. He studied the journey times and where each train he was riding should have been at a given moment. He was a human timetable and he would look out of the window and mutter, 'Hm . . . three minutes late at Bletchley,' or 'He'll never make it up to be on time at Stockport.' On one occasion we were travelling to an engagement in Leeds and the train was running very late indeed. Syd sat in the corner looking at his watch and muttering to himself, and as we ran into the station he said, 'This train driver is certainly no golf enthusiast . . . we'll only have time for nine holes.' I looked at him. 'What are you talking about?' I asked. 'We can't possibly go out to play now, there won't be enough light to finish.' He replied, 'Oh, come on . . . let's grab a taxi and get out to the course.'

There was no stopping him, so I reluctantly agreed, and we arrived at the clubhouse, complete with suitcases, violin, band parts, and golf clubs. He was out on the tenth tee taking a practice swing even before I had taken off my overcoat, and we started to play. We actually had to run between shots and by the time we teed up at the eighteenth, visibility was practically down to zero. He took the honour and swung his club, and the ball disappeared into the darkness. I took my swing and gave the ball a thump and we shouldered our bags and walked down the fairway. 'You went to the left, Ted,' said Syd. 'And I think I faded mine a bit to the right.' Miraculously this statement was correct, and we found both balls. 'Come on, Ted,' boomed Sydney's voice from the gloom, 'it's your shot.' 'But where *is* it?' I shouted. 'I can't see the green.' 'Oh,' he replied, '*Play six yards left of the moon!*'

When Syd left this life for the fairways of Elysium, Charlie Chester took me in his car to the cemetery. It didn't occur to me at the time, but as we came away, I remarked that I hadn't recognized too many of the mourners' faces. We drove out into the main road, and were held up by a fleet of cars leaving another cemetery near by. The faces of several people in the cars were very familiar. 'Charlie,' I said, 'do you know what I think?' 'Yes I do,' replied Chester. 'We've been to the wrong funeral.' 'In that case,' I said, 'I hope ours was also a golfer.'

9. THE GIPSY LIFE

Most golf pros will tell you that's it's a good idea to loosen up before starting a round. They advise one to swing a couple of clubs a dozen or so times before attempting to play. It's supposed to take out all the kinks and twinges and turn your quarter swing into a half swing.

I'm not so sure that it's a good idea. I know a golfer who was short on confidence. One Saturday morning he entered for the Captain's Prize, signed the entrance form and paid his sweep money, then went to the first tee, took a practice swing and promptly tore up his card. That's defeatism if you like.

Personally I never get there early enough to practise, and it usually takes me about four holes before I can connect solidly with the ball. A few years ago I decided to do something about it, and during a Summer Season in Blackpool I had an inspiration. I would buy a caravan and park it near the local golf course and then I would be there before the others arrived, and even if I couldn't get on a golf course I would be living in the country and communing with Nature.

So I bought a caravan, and *what* a caravan. It wasn't so much a caravan as a luxury flat on wheels. Fitted furniture and carpets, wall-bracket lights, a kitchen range and cold cupboard, in fact every convenience. Yes, it even had one of those! It cost over £2,000. I took delivery of it on the last day of the Summer Season, and towed it to Bradford for the commencing date of a Provincial tour.

On the way to the theatre coming into Bradford I passed a big restaurant, which was owned by a man named Harry Ramsden, and I later discovered that he specialized in fish and chips, which everyone knows is a theatrical performers' staple diet. There was a huge car-park, and I thought, 'This'll do,' and parked the van. Ramsden was an amiable man and at once agreed to let me stand my home on wheels next to the restaurant. I wondered why I hadn't thought of this before. No more hotels, complete privacy and saving money into the bargain. All through the two shows on Monday I was thinking, 'Tonight I'll close the door and cook myself a nice steak and with a half bottle of Burgundy it will be marvellous.'

I motored back to the caravan and I was just about to put the steak under the grill when a knock came at the door. I opened it and there stood a young man holding a tray on which was a covered dish. 'Mr Ramsden's compliments, sir,' he said, and vanished. It was a dish of steaming fish and chips and beautifully cooked. I put the steak back in the cold cupboard and got to work on my supper, which was most enjoyable. I thought of my brother and sister artistes in their second-rate hotels and heaved a sigh of contentment.

Unfortunately, the following morning I had a sad experience. I was in the habit of wearing a wedding ring which my dear wife had bought for me and on the inside was an inscription which read *To Ted from Sybil with love.* I couldn't grip the club very comfortably when wearing this ring, so I used to take it off and put it in my trouser pocket. Like lots of other golfers, I carried tee-pegs in my pocket which is a very bad habit. Unfortunately the sharp ends of the pegs had made a small hole in my pocket, the existence of which I was not then aware. At the end of the round I discovered the loss of the ring, and you can imagine how unhappy I was. I duly reported the matter to the secretary but without much hope of ever seeing the ring again.

My misery continued all evening and as I drove out to the caravan I didn't feel very hungry. After a while, however, I decided that I would have to eat something, and I took out the steak just as a knock came at the door, and there stood the young man with the tray. 'Mr Ramsden's compliments, sir,' he smiled, and handed it over. Fish and chips all hot and so I put my steak away again and got out the vinegar. The same thing happened every night. I tried coming home by a different route but it was of no avail. I thought of bolting the door or climbing under the bed, but I couldn't be so churlish. After all, it was a very kind gesture on the part of Harry Ramsden, who incidentally was charging me no rent at all. I thought of going behind a hedge and digging a tunnel as the prisoners of war did with the wooden horse, but abandoned the idea as impracticable.

On Saturday night I thought I would have to tell the young man that I wanted my steak, which had been in and out of the cupboard more times than my dad's fiddle had been in and out of the pawnshop. Then came the usual knock at the door. I opened it. 'Now look here . . .' I began and stopped. It was not the young man, it was another fellow altogether. 'Mr Ray?' he inquired, and I admitted that I had that honour. 'Here's your ring,' he said, and I took it from him. 'But how . . . where?' I asked. 'I've been pulling my tee shots,' he said. 'This morning I was playing from the rough and saw a glint of metal as I was playing my shot. The secretary told me of your loss and where you were.' I was staggered. The odds of anyone finding that ring were incalculable. I thanked him warmly and he turned to go. 'I must stop hooking my tee shots,' he muttered. 'Go and have a lesson on Monday,' I cried. 'I'll pay, and by the way, if you will wait for ten minutes, you can have some lovely fish and chips.'

10. THE STRAIGHT LEFT ARM

Everyone has seen photographs of the top-class pros. 'Frozen' at the end of the backswing. The left knee is bent, the right leg is straight and the left arm is like a ramrod. Don't try it, you'll be wasting your time and it will put back your game ten years. It's not for us. Mind you I'm not saying that it wouldn't look nice, but we just haven't the physical equipment.

And really it is a very recent cult. Look at some of the old golf books and you'll see what I mean. I have some pictures of a gentleman named Fred Robson, and at the top of his swing he appears to be trying to drive his back collar stud right through his neck with the shaft of the club. It is a beautiful picture and his left arm is not straight. And anyone who knows anything about golf will tell you that Fred Robson was one of the greatest teachers of all time. When most of the top professionals could be found in the bar, moaning about their lack of form and crying into their beer, Fred would offer words of balm and heal their wounds in a ten-minute session on the practice ground.

Ask anyone who the greatest-ever stylist was and he will say, seven times out of ten, 'Why, Harry Vardon, of course.' I have pictures of Harry Vardon, too, and they're just like Fred Robson's. Beautiful. What did Harry Vardon think of the so-called 'straight left arm'? Someone once asked him. Harry smiled. 'Bring him to me,' he said. 'That's the man I want to play, the man with the straight left arm.'

All of this leads me into the sad story of Jim, a victim if ever there was one. He played about six times a week and even went to the big tournaments to see how the champs did it. For Jim had a built-in *hook*. He hooked everything, and worked out a theory that if he could build up his left arm he would stop, once and for all, the horrible vicious duck-dive into the rough on the left that was keeping him awake at night and costing him money by day. In time he became imbued with the idea that if he could keep his left arm rigid with the wrists cocked, the head still and a pivot of ninety degrees, his troubles would be over. Unfortunately Jim stood only 5 feet 4 inches. He hadn't seen his feet for years, and he got winded when he tied his shoelaces. He got nowhere on his own and so he decided to go to the pro; but not just *one* pro, in the end, almost all of them. They were kind and spent lots of time in trying to help him, but really they could see that it was hopeless.

There came the time when Jim had almost run out of pros. Desperately he stopped his car on the road one day, outside a small and unfashionable club in the South. He found the pro, and hooked him for a lesson immediately. 'Fine,' said the pro. 'What's your trouble?' 'I want to keep my left arm straight,' replied Jim. 'OK,' said the teacher. 'Let's have a look at your swing.' Jim obliged. 'Well,' he asked. 'What do you think?' The pro had gone white. 'Do that again,' he managed to say.

Jim did so. 'I'm very sorry,' said the pro. 'But there is nothing I can do for you. If you want to be a happy man, never touch a golf club again.'

As he turned away, Jim grabbed his arm. 'I don't believe it,' he said. 'I have had lessons from some of the greatest, but you are the first man who has had the complete honesty to tell me I am wasting my time—please accept this.' And from his pocket he took out a roll of banknotes that would have choked a pig. The pro's eyes shot out like organ stops. 'Now let's not be hasty,' he gasped. 'Maybe if we take this very gradually . . .'

Jim kept at it, but got no better. He tried everything to build up his left side, hand and arm. He lifted heavy weights, bought a hand-spring gadget that he kept in his left-hand pocket and squeezed for hours. This often got him into trouble and on three occasions he was asked to leave the cinema. He bought a bicycle and removed the right handle bar and pedal and rode for miles every evening in the abortive attempt to develop his left side.

It was no use; every time he played he had the same horrible hook he had when he had first taken up the game. He hooked everything . . . even putts, and even made history by becoming the first man to hook a 'Shank'.

Driving through a town one day he was held up in a traffic jam. Immediately in front of his car was a huge Corporation dust cart and a giant coloured man was picking up some dustbins and, with a swing upwards, was emptying them into the cart. Jim couldn't believe his eyes. The chap had the perfect golf swing. Jim got out and approached him. 'Look here,' he said. 'If you'll show me how you do that I'll give you a quid.' The man eyed him suspiciously but Jim insisted. 'Go on,' he said, 'I mean it.' For the next ten minutes Jim was given a lesson in emptying dustbins. He told me later that it seemed to be the answer to his golfing problems and he could hardly wait for his first real attempt. Following his teacher's instructions, he took a firm grip and swung the heavy container over his shoulder. 'What happened, Jim?' I asked. 'You won't believe it, Ted,' he replied sadly, 'but I hooked the bloody dustbin.'

Hooked the bloody dustbin . . .

It wouldn't surprise me if you don't believe what I have written, but it is all true. There have been worse cases. Some have become hysterical and been taken away in strait-jackets. Have you ever seen one being worn? *Both* arms are bent.

Maybe some time you might like to discuss this with me further. Perhaps I'll see you in my local. You will notice that as I lift the pint to my lips my right arm will be bent. It is the only way known to man to slake his thirst. You can't do it with a straight left arm. In fact the only time my left arm is straight on such a happy occasion is when it's digging into my left-hand pocket to pay for my round. Cheers!

11. WHAT'S IN A NAME?

Words are wonderful things. Did you ever pause to realize that the funniest scripts in the world are all contained in a dictionary? The trick is, of course, that you have to assemble them in the proper order.

It's the same with people's names. Once you have become used to the pseudonym, the original is oftimes difficult to accept. A few examples ... Tony Curtis is really Bernie Schwartz, Cary Grant was originally Archibald Alexander Leach, and Gerry Dorsey was getting nowhere fast until he changed his name to Engelbert Humperdinck, and before I took the name of a great golfer called 'TED RAY' I was Charlie Olden. Mind you I wasn't christened 'Charlie Olden'. It was actually 'Charlie-BLAST IT-Olden'. Apparently the vicar stubbed his toe on the font. I didn't like my name very much and, although I loved my father and my mother, I never quite forgave them for starting me off in life with a name like that. I regretted that my father hadn't possessed a name like 'Blair-Paxton'; a name that, to me, had a lot of class. I couldn't for the life of me imagine that a name like 'Charlie Olden' would ever draw people into a theatre.

Make no mistake, even at the tender age of twelve I knew that I was going to be a comedian. At school I got more laughs (and more whoppings) than any kid you ever saw! Later in life, when I had broken into Show Business (actually it was more of a burglary) I reversed my surname and called myself 'NEDLO', but this name didn't get me anywhere either so I called myself 'HUGH NEEK'. Can you believe it? One evening when being announced as the winner of a so-called 'Talent' Contest, a short-sighted compère introduced me as 'Hush Week'! I bought him a pair of glasses and changed my name to 'Ted Ray'.

I got this name from a *Sportsmans' Diary* after a shrewd London agent demanded that I find a new 'Monicker', as it was called in *The Profession*. TED RAY, the man whose name I took, and whom I never met, was a formidable pro golfer from the Channel Isles, and he could heave a ball out of the deepest rough you ever saw, with a mashie-niblick which in those horrendous hands made the club look as though he was holding a toothpick. He wore a poacher's hat and a bush moustache, and a permanent pipe jutted from his jaws. They say that his swing would shake the foundations on adjacent council flats.

Tom Webster, the famous *Daily Mail* cartoonist of those days, had some wonderful stories about Ted Ray. Like the time he was inveigled into giving a lesson to some desperate member of the Oxhey Golf Club of which Ted was the pro. Apparently Ted hated giving tuition but he had promised to do so and he and the eager 'rabbit' approached the practice ground.

'All right, mate,' growled Ted (apparently he called everybody 'mate'). 'Let's see you hit one.' The pupil swung the club and sent the ball straight down the fairway to a distance of, perhaps, 180 yards. 'Well,' asked Ted. 'What's wrong with that, mate?' and the golfer said, 'Yes, but how do you hit them farther?' Ted looked at him. 'Hit them a bloody sight harder,' he snorted, and believe it or not, there ended the lesson!

But he must have been some golfer, this Ted Ray. Defying all the principles of the game, and with a tremendous sway on his backswing, he would heave his considerable girth at the ball, and finishing on his left heel with the toe pointing to the sky, he would thrash the ball as straight as an arrow to the middle of the fairway up to 300 yards away. And that wasn't all. His short game had all the delicacy of an old lady doing her needlework, and on the greens he appeared to be putting with a ball-point pen. On the occasions when he found trouble, his tremendous strength was more than equal to cope. His recovery shots were quite incredible. Bobby Jones described how, in his youth, he had seen Ted Ray play a ball from an unbelievably bad lie. A lie from which even a skylark would have found difficulty in getting airborne.

He brought down those tremendous hands on to a ball that no one else but he could see, and carried a small forest to send the ball flying like a buzzard and dropping lifelessly on to the green, which was some 150 yards away. Bobby Jones said that it was the greatest shot he has ever seen and I believe him.

Ted Ray was good enough to win the British Open in 1912 and the US Open in 1920. In his later years a newspaper tried to arrange a match between us for Charity. Unhappily it didn't materialize and I have always regretted it. I have also regretted the fact that we never met.

Ted Ray has been a lucky name for me. A few years ago, when I was appearing in my Radio Series 'Ray's a Laugh', a lady named Mrs Frank Forge sent me a letter. Apparently she had a souvenir

Carried a small forest . . .

of Ted Ray's in her possession, and she thought that I might be interested. She lived near Watford and I drove over to see her. She invited me into her immaculate little front parlour and pointed to an exquisite ornamental French clock that graced her mantelpiece, and apparently it had been presented to her dear departed, who had been Ted Ray's assistant, by Ted's widow.

Mrs Forge was about to move to retirement on the South Coast, and she said that as she was getting older she wanted the clock to pass into the hands of someone who would cherish it. 'Your name is Ted Ray,' she smiled, 'so who better?' I can tell you I choked a bit. I still have that clock, and it stands on the mantelpiece in my lounge. It has a gold plate on which is inscribed 'Presented to Ted Ray by the Oxhey Golf Club, to commemorate his winning the American Open Golf Championship 1920'.

I show it with pride to my visitors. I see them raise their eyebrows and I know what they are thinking. 'Doesn't he wear remarkably well for his age?' Then they see me play and they say, 'Oh dear, hasn't he gone off?'

Sic Transit something or other!

12. THE 'HUMPERS'

The golf-bag humper, or caddie, to give him his correct title, is vanishing from the golfing scene as fast as the North American Indian is from the United States. Americans now live in a world of manual and electric golf trolleys and, in the United States and even on certain courses in Britain, golfers are introducing little battery-powered go-carts that convey the owner and his friends from tee to green.

It's a pity really. A good caddie is worth his weight in gold, and I am sure that most of them regard the trolley as a mortal enemy, just as a lavatory attendant cannot be expected to gaze with friendship on a towel cabinet. There is nothing the caddie can do about it, of course. They have no Union, as far as I know, and they live a gipsy-like existence. At one time, some of them actually spent the nights before a big match sleeping in hedge-rows, while others, in winter, when not much was going on in big golf, would actually get themselves 'pinched' on some mild charge that would guarantee them the warmth of a cell and three meals a day. Of course this is all in the distant past, and caddies these days are noticeably cleaner and better dressed.

I shall never forget the day when a friend of mine turned up at Walton Heath with a brand-new golf trolley. The others in the four-ball, including myself, had booked caddies and, as we stood on the first tee, an unemployed 'humper' glowered at my friend, who unwrapped a ball and placed it on the tee. I am sure that he was a bit put off by the basilisk glare that was boring into the back of his head, because he produced the father-and-mother of a slice which sent his ball flying high and deep into the trees on the right. The caddie sneered. 'Let the bleedin' trolley go and find that!' he shouted. I had to laugh.

I know quite a few of the professional bag-carriers and they usually have an amusing story to tell when I see them at some Tournament or other. Like old 'Wiry' whom I met at the Penfold Tournament a year or two ago. 'It was like this, Mr Ray,' said Wiry. 'There's this amateur who thought he was a lot better'n he was, and he's playing the pro for two dozen balls. Well, as soon as I seen his backswing I knew he had no chance, and the pro hands him a Dog's Licence and it's all over at the twelfth. This mug, although you wouldn't believe it, actually asks the pro if he'll have six rollers on the bye and Muggins gets done again to the tune of three and two and on the seventeenth tee, he looks at me and says, "Well, caddie, shall we have a ball on the bye-bye?" "No," I says. "Let's have one on the ruddy fairway!"'

Yes they are an amusing lot. If you play a good shot, they use the Royal 'We'. '*We* did it, sir,' '*We've* played it, sir,' '*We* hit a good 'un there, sir,' etc. But just foozle it, and you're on your own. 'YOU made a right mess of that one, guv'nor!'

Caddies *always* give me an inferiority complex. I remember a tall gangling man who carried my clubs in a competition and at the first short hole I hooked my tee shot and put it in some bushes to the left of the green. The caddie looked at me. 'You got that one labelled?' he asked. I nodded. We reached the spot where I thought my ball had entered the hedge. We didn't find it. He gave me a withering look. 'I thought you said you had it labelled,' he said. I was so frightened I almost apologized! My partner that day was not so easily intimidated. His caddie just laughed every time my friend made a bad shot, which I might say was frequently. Finally Jack turned to the bag-carrier and said threateningly, 'One more laugh out of you and I'll swipe you over the head with this four wood!' 'Ah,' replied the caddie. 'But not if you take a full swing!'

During a Ladies' County Championship a caddie came back into the Pro Shop. 'What are you doing here, Fred?' asked the pro. 'Well, sir,' replied the caddie. 'I was carrying the bag for Mrs Wotherspoon and just as we were coming to the fourth, a hen ran across the course chased by a big red cock. Now he'd almost caught her when he suddenly stopped and picked up a worm. Well, sir. I happened to look at Mrs Wotherspoon and I said, "Blimey, Missus, I hope I never get as hungry as that." Then she three-putted and sent me back to the clubhouse.'

Most caddies are honest, but some are not beyond using the 'leather mashie' (that is a little nudge with the boot when the ball is in a deep lie). Of course even these few would only resort to that measure when the game is just a friendly and his man is having a bad time. I played at a course just outside Birmingham and I put my ball right behind a tree. 'I wouldn't have fancied this lie in a medal,' I remarked. 'If this had been a medal, guv'-nor,' grinned my caddie, 'you wouldn't have had it!'

When caddies are good, they are very good. One of our top pros was playing Wentworth and he pulled his ball into the rough. 'What do I need here?' he asked the Humper. 'A four iron,' came the answer. The pro took his advice and played the shot. It

The Leather Mashie . . .

wasn't a very good one so he threw the club back to the caddie and said, 'You gave me the wrong club . . . call yourself a caddie?' Without hesitation the caddie dropped a ball in the identical spot from where the pro had just played and taking the four iron, played a perfect shot right to the heart of the green. 'When you can do that,' he remarked to the astonished professional, 'you can call yourself a flippin' golfer.'

As I remarked earlier in this chapter, caddies today are generally better groomed than those of yesteryear. One who certainly wasn't was the poor blighter who carried the clubs of that great comedian Monsieur Eddy Gray some time ago, when we contested a final of a theatrical golfing competition at Sudbury. This caddie was really a sight to behold, a greasy cap with bunches of hair peeping through, and a shattered pair of plimsolls from which protruded his toes. I don't know how I ever managed to concentrate on a shot during that round. Eddy Gray was so funny. I managed to win the game at the seventeenth and Eddy shook my hand. 'Thanks for the game, mate,' he grinned. 'I've been in twelve finals and never won one.' He then turned to his caddie and tripped him up and shoved him on his back into the long grass. 'It's all your fault,' he shouted. The poor disreputable caddie looked up. 'Why, what have I done?' he asked plaintively. 'Ah shut up,' said Eddy. 'You Americans are all alike!'

13. THE YORKSHIRE TERRIER

As I have often said, Golf was invented to while away the lonely hours of touring comics and keep them out of the taverns. It took them from pubs to pastures, where they could concentrate on sinking putts instead of pints. So it was with pleasure that one sunny morning in Edinburgh I had a telephone call in my hotel bedroom from a fellow-comedian by name Duggie Wakefield who told me that he was motoring across from Glasgow to Edinburgh to play a friendly round with me on the Royal Burgess Golf Club at Barnton, reputedly the second oldest golf club in the British Isles.

Now Duggie was not only the proud bearer of a good old Yorkshire surname, but he really was a 'Tyke' born and bred and I am sure that if you had cut his veins he would have bled pudding! We had played many games of golf together and on sunny mornings we foregathered at the pleasant Hendon Golf Club, on the border of which Duggie lived.

On one occasion we were appearing together at the Finsbury Park Empire where the audiences were so friendly that you would have had to rehearse to 'flop'! Duggie and his gang were performing his hilarious motor-car sketch which was so funny that it always had to close the first half of the show, immediately before the interval, because nothing could follow it.

After our golf game at Hendon we drove off to the theatre and suddenly Duggie turned to me and said, 'Did you know that Hal Roach was coming to see the show tonight?' I must admit that my pulse quickened a trifle. Hal Roach was at that time possibly the top comedy producer in Hollywood, and at once I conjured up visions of a nice fat contract which would take me to Los Angeles and possible fame and fortune. I called myself 'The Machine Gun of Gagsters' at that time, and though you may think that was going a bit far, I really could fire out the 'one-liners', as we call the quick jokes, with the best of them. I knew that Roach could be interested in only three of the acts on the bill. Duggie, of course, Jack Barty (a burly cockney comic) and me. There was another comedian on the bill but he was crude and rude and, frankly, I couldn't see him as a potential film star.

I discovered that the great Hollywood producer would be attending the first house performance that evening and directly the curtain was up and the opening dog-act was sniffing and cocking its way through the routine tricks, I took a furtive peep from the wings and sure enough there on the very front row sat Hal Roach whom I recognized from his pictures in the movie magazines. He was flanked by two other Americans with large, flowing flowered neckties.

The dogs finished their performance and trotted off, and the second-turn comic made his entrance and went into his routine, churning out the gags that were fraying at the edges. I took another look at Roach and his two friends and even from where I was standing I could see that their eyes had taken on a glazed look. The comic (if you will pardon the expression) mercifully came to the end of his patter, and shuffled off to a mere trickle of applause.

A 'Sister' act followed. Blonde and brassy, and slightly passé, but they belted out their numbers with gusto, and they both had lovely legs. The audience loved them, and even joined in the choruses.

Jack Barty's number went into the frame and he had the audience with him from the start. Dressed in a striped blazer, grey flannels and a straw boater, he told his gags crisply and his patter was as clean as a whistle. Hal Roach and his friends laughed as heartily as anyone, and gave Jack a warm hand at the end of his act.

'They're *pie* tonight, Ted,' said Jack as he came off. 'You'll knock 'em for six.'

I returned to my dressing-room because the next two acts consisted of a Puppet Show and a Bosomy Soprano and I was certain that Hal Roach hadn't come 6,000 miles to see them! Duggie Wakefield and his gang closed the first half with their 'sure-fire' motor-car sketch, a hit from Perth to Penzance.

In my dressing-room I was sitting in front of the mirror practising 'double-takes', 'slow-burns' and all the grimaces I had seen on the silver screen, and suddenly the call-boy knocked on my door and said, 'Five minutes Mr Ray.'

I took my violin from its case and made my way to the stage. I felt great and really on form. The orchestra struck up my music and I entered to a welcoming round of applause. Unfortunately I hardly heard it. There were three empty stall seats on the front

58

row. Hal Roach and his friends had left. It didn't make me feel any better when I later discovered that, while I was performing out front, Hal Roach was talking to Duggie Wakefield in the latter's dressing-room. So vanished my one and only chance of getting to Hollywood. Not that for one moment I begrudged Duggie his big chance, because he was a good companion, an unselfish comedian, and he never pinched a joke in his life. He didn't have to, because he had one of the most naturally funny faces I have ever seen. Apparently Hal Roach thought so too. He told Duggie's agent, 'I'll put that face on the cinema screens of the world . . . I'll blow it up so that no one can miss it. That boy is going to be the funniest comedian in the business.'

So Duggie sailed for Hollywood, minus his gang, but with Jack Barty who had impressed Roach as a supporting character.

Let Duggie take over.

'Ted,' he told me, 'I have never seen anything like it. They gave me the full STAR treatment before they had even shot a single foot of film. I was wined and dined, housed in a luxury flat and every possible comfort was accorded me wherever I went. Finally we got on to the studio floor and began to shoot. Everyone laughed like "drains" and I couldn't have asked for finer writers or a more competent director, and we finished the film right on schedule. A few weeks passed and they decided to give the film a "sneak-preview" somewhere out of town. It was a disaster! Instead of the audience laughing when I appeared on the screen, the women in the audience shuddered. They just couldn't stand my face and, as you know, Ted, if you can't please the women, you're sunk. The film company made another try with me, but again it was a failure. Hal Roach realized that he had made a king-sized bloomer and a few days later I was summoned to the front office. "Wakefield," they said, "we're sorry that it hasn't worked out, but after all, anyone can make a mistake." "What does *that* mean?" I asked.

' "Well, Duggie, buddy, it's like this. We'd like to call it a day and we are willing to pay you off." "How much?" I asked. They mentioned a figure. "No thanks," I told them. "It isn't enough." The chief Mogul smiled. "Now look, boy," he said. "This deal isn't going to work out, now what do you want?" "The lot," I told him. "The full amount I was contracted for. After all, it isn't *my* fault if you made a mistake, is it?" '

Duggie paused for a moment. 'What happened?' I said. 'Well,'

Duggie went on. 'I went back to my paid-for Hollywood pad and sat there for a month on full salary. Came the day when the studio sent for me and told me that they contemplated making a comedy film that was rather unusual. Every character in the film was to be a dog. "It's a kind of fantasy," they said. "The leading lady is a poodle, the villain is a boxer, and you will be an Old English sheepdog. Now go down to make-up and we'll shoot the trial scenes." "Oh, a sheep-dog trial," I said, but nobody laughed. Well, I sat in that chair and they gave me a dog skin and proceeded to make up my face hair by hair. They put them on with meticulous precision and when they had finished and I looked at myself in the mirror I honestly believed that I could have won "best of breed" at Crufts! I went down to the set and they took a few "still" photographs and we broke for the day at 5 pm. I was on my way to the dressing-room when the director stopped me. "Just one thing baby," he said with a smile. "Don't remove the make-up, it takes a long time to put on and we are shooting very early in the morning." I could hardly believe this, but I had to go along with it, for after all, I had a contract and they had me over the proverbial barrel.

'I spent a most uncomfortable night but I was at the studio bright and early the next morning, determined not to give them the slightest loophole to cancel my agreement. They went through several "line-ups", tests and camera positions, but not a single frame of film was taken, when the cry came, "One hour . . . break for lunch."

'What a mockery that was for me. Have you ever tried eating yoghurt through a straw? Well, I had to live, didn't I? Back on the set for the afternoon, for the same "non-working" period and at the end of the day back to my lonely flat with the instruction "Don't touch the make-up!" All I could do was to sit there and watch TV. It was dreadful. When something funny happened on the screen, I didn't know whether to laugh or bark. The next day was the same, and the next and the next. I began to feel that I really *was* a dog and, when I visited the "loo", I automatically cocked my leg. It was impossible for me to find a partner on the golf course at weekends. Not that I could blame them really, looking as I did, so I just ploughed my lonely way around, to the occasional jeers of passers-by such as "It's dogged as does it", "He's barking up the wrong tree", and "You should see him play the dog-leg tenth."

'After a while I felt thin and ill, which was not surprising since no solid food had passed through my lips for a fortnight. Then the front office sent for me. "Wakefield," said the big boss, "we're going to call it a day . . . go to the cashier and get your money." And so I did,' concluded Duggie. 'And every bloody cent that was owing to me . . . and *why not*? I didn't ask them to take me to Hollywood . . . they asked *me*.'

And that's the story he told me on that sunny morning in Edinburgh. And every word of it is true.

I looked at him. Nine and a half stone of Yorkshire guts. And what guts. Resilience if ever I saw it.

There was a short silence. 'Well, come on Duggie,' I finally said, 'let's go out and play some golf.'

Now I don't know of a finer or more delightful golf course than the Royal Barnton and it's not really difficult. Rolling tree-lined fairways, and beautiful greens . . . in all, a most pleasant place in which to be. Even with all this, poor Duggie was right off form, and I had no difficulty in beating him handsomely.

'Oh dear,' he murmured as we walked to the nineteenth. 'It's entirely the fault of those hospitable Scots. They plied me with far too much whisky last night.' 'Never mind,' I consoled. 'Drink this and you'll feel much better.' Duggie took the glass. 'What is it?' he asked. 'Scotch of course,' I grinned. 'They say there's nothing better after a party than the Hair of the Dog!'

14. LESSONS FROM THE TOP

In my search for the perfect swing I have always been willing to take advice from anyone who thought he could help. I was appearing on a Music Hall Show and a friend of mine named Godfrey was on the bill. He performed a great dancing act with his sister and he was well over six feet tall and played a great game of golf. During a matinee one afternoon I told him of my poor form and he offered to help. 'When?' I asked. 'Now,' he replied. 'Bring a club and come upstairs.' This particular theatre had a flat roof, and Godfrey soon had me swinging away at an imaginary ball. 'There,' he said, after a quarter of an hour or so. 'Swing like that and you'll be OK.' 'Thanks, Godfrey.' I said. 'I can't wait to get to the course and try it.'

Godfrey thought for a minute. 'Well, there's no time like the present,' he said. 'What do you mean?' I inquired. He took a ball out of his pocket, stuck a tee peg into a crack in the cement and teed up the ball. 'Hit it,' he ordered. I looked around at the housetops. 'But it might land anywhere,' I protested. 'Oh, go on,' he snorted. 'Drive it across those railway lines.' I addressed the ball, swung back slowly, and let fly. I made a good contact and the ball took off straight and true, and flew straight through the open window of a signal box and out of a corresponding window on the other side. Godfrey and I were back in the dressing-room in ten seconds flat. I often laugh about the incident. But what about the bloke in the signal box? He must have thought that someone at Sunningdale had one hell of a slice!

They should award degrees to professional golfers. The teachers I mean. What therapeutic powers they must possess to iron out some of the crooked swings at a golf ball that are perpetrated by the misguided followers of the game. So why shouldn't the pro also have letters behind his name? Instead of MUS. BAC., why not SLOW BACK?

We have all been to various shrines to learn, and hopefully retain, the words of wisdom from the Greats. My own particular 'Scalps' include Cotton, Rees, Shankland, Daly, Whitcombe (Chas), Mitchell (Len), Faulkner (Max), and a pro named

Beldon. I felt most sorry for the last-named. More about him later!

Near the end of the Second World War, I discovered to my delight that I was to appear at the Empire Theatre, Nottingham, on the same bill with no less a person than Henry Cotton. 'This is it,' I thought. The end of all my worries. Surely during the forthcoming week I could elicit from him *'The Secret'*. Because I am convinced that it *does exist*.

They won't tell us, you know and, before you read on, I must put you out of your misery and tell you that Cotton didn't give it to me. He was charming in every other respect. He came to the theatre every morning (unfortunately it was in the depths of winter and snow covered the golf courses so that there was no chance of a 'knock') but Henry had a large net on the stage of the theatre which he used for his demonstrations, which were masterly. He was kind enough to give helpful hints, gratis, to anyone who was keen enough to try to improve his or her game. All the show people asked for help. On the Wednesday Henry agreed to give *me* a lesson. He'd become tired of seeing me on my knees. Gratefully I stepped up to the simulated grass mat. Cotton teed up a ball. 'Hit it,' he said. 'That's it,' I thought. 'The *Secret*.' Forget everything else . . . just *hit it*!'

Something must have gone wrong, because although the net was a large one, covering three sides of the stage, and facing the rear wall of the theatre, I actually broke a lamp in the footlights *behind me*! Henry was sympathetic. 'What are you trying to do?' he asked. 'Knock the cover off the ball? Swing the club and go through sweetly.' 'Ah, of course,' I thought. 'Graceful.' I tried again, the ball actually went straight forward. Unfortunately it didn't possess enough strength to reach the back of the net. 'Very nice,' said Cotton. 'An excellent impression of Pavlova the ballet dancer, but where's the vigour?'

Again and again I tried to put into practice the advice that the Maestro was giving me, but frankly there was little improvement. Finally even Henry had had enough. 'You'll have to do something about your hands,' he said. I looked at them. They seemed clean enough. No, it wasn't that. I realized that they weren't strong enough. Oh, I could caress the neck of a fiddle or hold a pint without spilling any, but it seems that to get anywhere in golf you must be able to crush rocks or bend bottle-tops between two fingers.

'Never mind,' consoled Cotton, 'I'll give you some publicity in my Sunday newspaper column.

He was as good as his word. The following Sunday I was up early and dashed across to the railway station to buy the paper and read what he had written. There it was, headlines too. 'THE VIOLINIST WITH THE PICCOLO GRIP.' Thanks Henry. I shall always think of you when I'm playing Beethoven's Fifth.

You couldn't meet a nicer bloke than Bill Shankland. He invited me over to Potters Bar to get the kinks out of my swing. Bill can see right away whether or not a player has promise. Me and Jacklin, for instance. I went to see Bill every Wednesday morning for three months. Finally he was satisfied. I will never forget his words when I arrived for my final day's tuition. 'You're a strong little devil,' he grinned. 'And as long as you never forget to pull that left hand through to the hole, you will play good golf.'

I then hit seventy-three perfect drives, shook hands with Bill, and went home. I was singing when I drove away and when I reached home I kissed my wife and gave her a fiver. The following Sunday was the day that the members of my club were to meet for the Captain's Prize. As I saw them lacing up their shoes in the locker-room I felt so sorry for them. 'Poor blighters,' I thought. 'Little do they realize that with my playing off my present handicap they have no chance.'

It was a beautiful day and on the first tee I took a couple of practice swings and then addressed the ball. Well, to be honest, balls. I hooked three brand-new ones, two of which I never saw again, clean out of bounds. Then I tore my card up, apologized to the other two players, and went straight into the bar. Thanks, Bill, anyway, you really tried.

Dai Rees, the fiery and talented Welsh pro, has written many fine instructional books on golf, and I have read most of them. However, one practical demonstration is worth all the writing in the world and on one occasion, when Dai was a guest on a radio show of mine, he showed me the golf swing in one of the dressing-rooms at the BBC and all he used was a rolled-up newspaper. Have you ever tried it? Don't waste your time. You can't hit a ball very far with a rolled-up newspaper.

Max Faulkner said, 'Flatten your swing, you can't swing flat enough.' No? You can if you keep on hitting your right kneecap on the backswing, and I've got the swollen cartilage to prove it!

One evening during a Summer Season at the Grand Theatre Blackpool I was informed that Fred Daly was in the audience. My act that night consisted of references to hooks, slices, and pitch shots to the green. Fred was greatly amused and received a tremendous 'hand' from the audience when I introduced him from the stage. The happy Irishman was on his way to Birkdale where he was to retain the Match-Play Championship. He came backstage to my dressing-room where I 'happened' to be toying with a sawn-off club that I used to practise swinging with between shows. Well, you see it was a very small dressing-room. Even the mice were round-shouldered!

Fred was kind enough to not only give me a quick lesson, but even to invite me to play a round of golf with him the following morning at the Old Links at Lytham St Annes. We made up a four-ball with Phil Rogers the club pro, and the then captain.

It was a beautiful summer morning when we teed off, and Fred and I were partners. I'm no fool!

It was a very pleasant game and as we reached the eighteenth tee, the news that Fred was there had got around and the last green was surrounded by about two hundred members of the club. At that time the eighteenth at the Old Links was a short hole of, say, 150 yards and we all hit good shots and found the green from the tee. It just so happened that Fred's ball was a couple of yards farther away from the hole than mine, which was a dozen yards or so away from the cup. In a very loud voice I said, 'You go for the safe three, will you, Fred, and I'll get the two.'

You won't believe it, but it's true. Fred laid his ball stone dead, and I slotted mine! I could hear the comments as I left the green. 'Who *is* he? No, not Daly, the *other* one?'

Finally Ernie Beldon. A nice little unheard-of pro in Yorkshire. I was playing a theatre in Bradford and one morning popped out to the course to put in a bit of practice. I went into his shop to buy some balls. 'How's your golf?' he inquired. 'Well, so-so,' I replied. 'Except for the loop I have at the top of my swing.' I wasn't kidding. You never saw such a loop. You could have rounded up cattle with it. 'Come down tomorrow,' said Beldon. 'I'll take a look at you.' I was there the next day and the lesson began. After a few swings he said, 'You're making things difficult for yourself. Just take the club back inside the line and bring it down smoothly to the ball.' I tried. By golly I tried.

'Don't worry,' said Beldon. 'It may take a little time, come back tomorrow.'

I did, I also visited him the next day, and the next. On the Friday Beldon didn't seem very pleased to see me 'I can't understand you,' he almost growled. 'There are old ladies in this club who can swing the club properly, why the hell can't you?' 'I'm trying,' I protested. 'All right then,' he said, 'come on and we'll have another go.'

After an hour he was shouting at me and practically shook me by the throat. 'What's the matter with you?' he yelled. 'I think you're doing it on purpose.' 'No I'm not,' I protested. 'I just want to improve my game.' He glowered at me. 'When does your show leave Bradford?' he asked. 'Tomorrow,' I said. Beldon breathed very hard. 'A day too late,' he said and walked away.

I returned to the theatre and I didn't see Beldon again for two years. It was at Moortown in a big tournament. He didn't play very well, and missed qualifying for the final two rounds by eight strokes. I wasn't surprised really. You never saw a swing with such a loop in it in your life!

15. THE 'WEAKER' SEX

A friend of mine was playing on a strange course, and as he was addressing his ball, the helpful secretary opened the window of his office and shouted, 'Excuse me, but you are playing from the Ladies' Tee!' My friend replied, 'You mind your own blasted business, I'm playing my ninth.'

Most golf courses look very attractive from the Ladies' Tees, and as we get on in years, we can all use that extra thirty yards. After all, women are supposed to be the weaker sex, but I've met a few who gave the lie to this assumption.

There was the time I met up with a pro in Blackpool. He had a little Club where you could enjoy a quiet drink, and there was an indoor net where he gave lessons, and one evening he asked me if I fancied a few holes at the North Shore links. I said, 'Great, I'll see you there at nine thirty in the morning.'

The next day at a quarter to ten, a healthy and rather plump lady arrived and said, 'I'm sorry, but Jack can't make it, so do you mind if I play instead?'

I took a poor view of Jack at that moment. 'What a liberty!' I thought, but of course I couldn't be rude, and I said, 'Fine. I'm twelve handicap, what are you?' 'Oh, I'm four,' she answered, and I must admit that this took the smile off my face. 'Well, I don't know much about women's handicaps,' I said. 'How do we work out the shots?' 'Well,' she said sweetly. 'Suppose I play from the men's tees and give you four strokes, will that be all right?'

Well, I must admit that this made me grin. A little plump woman like that offering to me, eleven stone of muscle and whipcord, four strokes ... it was too ridiculous. 'Your honour,' I said. 'Ladies first.' She teed up a ball and bisected the fairway with her drive, and the shot must have been every inch of 220 yards. It shook me a bit and I put a little more into my drive than I would otherwise have done. After a few minutes we found my ball in the rough, where I could only hack it out and as she laid her second near the flag, I was one down. Then I was two down, and then three down and the match was over at the fourteenth, where she had handed me a lacing to the tune of six up and four to play.

I shook hands with her and said, 'Would you like a drink?' 'Thank you, no,' she replied. 'I have to give a lesson at twelve-thirty.' She got into her car and drove off, and that was the last I ever saw of her. I haven't seen Jack again either and I can't say I'm sorry. I don't really bear a grudge, but isn't it silly that a woman can make you feel so inadequate on the course? I've seen, met, and played some wonderful women players. Jacqueline Gordon, Marley Spearman, and others, so lovely to watch, with perfect swings.

Interesting about Marley. Her husband was a very keen golfer and one day she asked him if she could go along and see what the game was all about. Marley was a professional dancer, as willowy as a soft-shafted golf club, and as feminine as they come. She walked around the course and got interested and her hubby gave her a club and said, 'All right, just knock the ball about and have fun.' She knocked the ball about all right, and what started as fun led her to win the British Ladies' Championship, among other triumphs.

Pam Barton and Bridget Newell too. I saw them contest the National Final at Southport and Ainsdale, and admired their skill so much, little realizing at the time that they were both to die so tragically and prematurely; Biddy while practising for a tournament, and little Pam in a flying accident during the Second World War. Babe Zaharias, who could hit the ball way past Jacqueline Gordon who could leave *me* twenty yards. Why ever did I take up this game? Babe Didrikson Zaharias's unavailing fight against a malignant disease is one of the greatest 'fight-backs' in the history of the game, and she deservedly won The Ben Hogan Trophy in 1953—the greatest come-back of the year.

Joyce Wethered had a swing that was described by the great Bobby Jones as the greatest ever. What a player she must have been! And it is on record that even the scream of a passing train-whistle couldn't make her look up when she had a vital putt.

Asked afterwards why it hadn't put her off, she simply said, 'I didn't hear it.' Oh to possess such concentration! I get put off when a butterfly flies by, three fairways away.

Anyway, let's not be patronizing to the women. I was playing at North Foreland and noticed an attractive young girl on the practice ground. 'That's a very nice little swing, my dear,' I

remarked. 'Carry on that way and you will become a good player.'
'Thank you, sir,' she said, and the following week she went out
and won the Girls' Championship. Her name was Angela Ward
and she was to become Mrs Michael Bonallack, and play for
Britain in the Curtis Cup and win lots of Championships. She
laughed when I reminded her of the occasion.

My own wife, Sybil, has a lovely swing, although she doesn't
play. I took her out once to the Bishopbriggs course at Glasgow
and fixed her up with some clubs, and partnered her up with the
wife of a fellow-comedian. This was when we were appearing at
the Empire Theatre in Sauchiehall Street.

Eddie and I finished our round and sat on the verandah of the
clubhouse enjoying a friendly pint. Eventually Sybil and Lila
appeared and as they came up the eighteenth fairway, one
couldn't help but notice that they weren't exactly walking arm
in arm. Sybil's face was red and I could see that she was upset.
'Would you care for a drink, dear?' I inquired. 'No thank
you,' she snapped. 'Let's get going.' I looked at Eddie and
shrugged my shoulders and we climbed in the car and drove back
to town.

'Whatever happened?' I asked. 'That woman,' breathed Sybil.
'What a cheat. You know that little hole across the bridge just
before the last one? Well, she said she only had seventeen shots
but I counted nineteen myself. I will never play with her again.'
And do you know something? She never did!

But she still loves the game and walks around the fairways
with me at lots of the big tournaments. I guess she must be the
only woman in Britain who has walked around three full eighteen
holes at Gleneagles, once round the Queen's Course and TWICE
round the King's in the same day! I know I've said that before
but I like to talk about it.

Once I was appearing at the Queen's Theatre, South Shields,
and on the bill was a Hungarian pickpocket-conjuror. He saw the
bag of clubs in my dressing-room. 'What's your handicap?' he
asked. 'Ten,' I said. 'Oh, I'm only five,' he replied. 'How long have
you been playing?' I inquired. 'Only for three weeks,' he said. 'I
play at Hendon.'

I thought this rather unusual, to say the least, but there was
only one way to find out and so the next day we went out to the
course. It was very foggy and on the first tee, I remember just
seeing him swish the club and he marched off. Eventually, after

shouts and whistles across the mist we met up again on the first green. 'How many have you had?' I queried. 'Two,' came the reply. 'Oh,' I said. 'I've had four, it's your hole.'

The fog didn't lift but somehow we finished the round. 'What's he like?' asked Sybil that evening. 'I really don't know,' I replied honestly, 'I've never seen him play.'

The next day Sybil went with us. 'I'll walk round with him,' she said. We drove off. His ball shot off at a tangent about forty-five degrees to the right. He took a swing and missed. 'Two,' said Sybil. He glared at her and took another vicious swipe and failed to make contact with the ball. 'Three,' said Sybil calmly. 'No, no,' protested the conjuror. 'We don't count those!' '*We do,*' said Sybil. 'You're playing four.'

I felt a bit sorry for the Hungarian conjuror. He went round in one hundred and twenty-two. Poor blighter, the game's difficult enough without walking around with a female computer. He gave me the half-crown, and I said, 'Let's have a game at your course some time. Did you say it's Hendon?' He nodded. 'And your handicap is five?' I asked. 'Yes,' he answered. 'In that case,' I said, 'you must always start at the fifteenth!'

16. THE ROAD TO MAIDENHEAD

In 1952 I had a phone call from my old friend Donald Peers. Donald is a fine golfer, and has actually played in the Amateur Championship. His performance was not memorable, but then again, it's tough at the top. Donald swings the club sweetly and even from the back tees he is often twenty or thirty yards beyond the 200-yard marker. His short game, like his singing, is immaculate and precise. Yes, Donald is a very good golfer and I think he holds a record that has never been equalled. You may not find it in the Guinness Book of Records but nevertheless it is true. He did four successive holes in 1, 2, 3, and 4 shots respectively. Two eagles, a birdie, and a par in four holes. How about that?

'What's on your mind, Donald?' I inquired. 'Would you like to make up a four-ball on Sunday week?' he asked. Now it just so happened that Sybil was visiting her mother on that day so I accepted gratefully. 'Where is it, Donald?' I asked, and Donald said, 'It's at the Temple Golf Course at Maidenhead, and it's a Charity Exhibition Game in aid of the Duke of Edinburgh's Playing Fields Association.'

I was very excited. 'Thanks very much for asking me,' I replied, and hung up ... Then came the reaction. An exhibition game ... I mean, me and my short game! I have seldom had qualms with the long shots ... but the pitch and run ... the wedge, and all those little shots around the green. My heart sank. 'Tomorrow,' I thought, 'I will have to phone Donald and tell him that it's off.'

The next morning at breakfast Sybil passed me the morning papers. 'You've got a mention,' she remarked. There it was in headlines, on the sports pages:

'DONALD PEERS AND TED RAY TO PLAY EXHIBITION MATCH FOR CHARITY AGAINST BING CROSBY AND BOB HOPE'

I felt ill! I put the top back on the boiled egg and said, 'Save that till Wednesday.' I wanted to go back on my promise, but what could I do? It was no use, I was saddled with it. I just couldn't let Donald down.

Honestly, I didn't have a good night's sleep for the next eight days, if you get my meaning. On the Saturday immediately before the game, I had an inspiration. I rang up Bill Cox, the famous pro at Fulwell, and told him of my worries. 'Can I come and see you today, Bill?' I pleaded. 'I'm really in trouble.' 'Why of course,' answered Bill. 'I'll reserve the practice ground for you at eleven o'clock.'

I got the car out of the garage and drove the twenty or so miles from my house to Bill's course. I told him about my problems and he said, 'Look, Ted, don't worry, don't get tense, just relax and take it easy. Now let me see you play a short chip shot.' I played six and foozled them all. 'What should I do, Bill?' I asked plaintively. 'Emigrate!' said Bill.

Sunday morning was bright and sunny. I had been praying all night for rain. Well, at least it would have cut down the crowds who were to see my misery. I got to the club and walked into the locker-room. There is something soothing about a locker-room, it seems to relax one. I wasn't really nervous, except for the fact, as I discovered later, that I laced up the golf shoes of a man who was just taking them off.

Donald Peers was already on the practice ground loosening up. I joined him. 'Hello, Ted,' smiled Donald. 'You look great.' I always was good at character parts. I hit a few balls and they all went away nicely. As I have already said, the long game to me, at least, has always been the easiest part of golf. It's just that I can't play those silly little chips around the green that any dear old lady can play with an umbrella.

There was no sign of Hope and Crosby. I subsequently discovered that they were on a neighbouring course getting in a bit of crafty practice.

The crowds were gathering. I finished my warm-up and walked to the clubhouse. Crosby and Hope arrived. Hope looked at me. 'Say, Bing,' he cracked. 'We can't possibly beat anyone who looks that healthy.' I laughed weakly. 'So you're Ted Ray,' said Bob. There was no point in denying it. 'Yes, that's right,' I said, flattered to think he knew me. 'Yes,' said Hope. 'Where were you playing last week?' 'Sham Castle,' I told him. 'That's near Bath.' 'Yes,' replied Bob, 'I went round the course after you and I was playing my ball out of your divots.'

'So it's going to be that sort of game,' I thought, and suddenly half the pressure came off.

We were called to the first tee, and in traditional manner we tossed for the honour. It's strange but there are still a lot of golfers who think that the lowest handicapped golfer should go first. Not true. The order of play is decided by lot. I took out a coin, tossed it, and Peers and I won. Well, Crosby and Hope had never seen a rouble!

The first hole at Temple is downhill. So should every first hole be. But this one looked different. Have you ever seen a golf hole that looks like a keyhole? This one did. The edges of the fairway were lined with people who spaced out around the green and framed the whole area. I took a deep breath and swung the club. The ball took off like a quail and bored the centre of the fairway as if it had been fixed by a computer. Hope looked at me with new respect. I was so pleased, I gave him back two of his gags!

The first hole was halved in four, as was the second. I thought that the crowds would embarrass me, but the reverse happened. And when I say Crowds, I really mean *Crowds*. Just about eleven thousand of them, a third of whom had paid, and four-fifths of whom had never seen a golf course in their lives! There were kids playing sand castles in bunkers, and smartly dressed ladies stamping their stiletto heels all over the beautiful greens, but I felt happy and relaxed.

Bob Hope drove his ball straight into the lens of a press camera at the fifth, smashing it beyond repair, and I told a lady to close her mouth as I had lost two balls already. It was that sort of game.

Crosby I found to be a kind and very gentle man. He was 'three' handicap and as we walked arm in arm down the fairway I noticed that he had his signature inscribed on all of his clubs. 'Don't tell me you actually manufacture golf clubs, Bing,' I said. 'Oh yes,' he replied with a grin, 'I'll do anything for money ... steal even.'

What a lovely bloke he turned out to be, and what a fine golfer. Unfortunately he, like myself, was getting worried about the encroachment of the spectators. The stewards just couldn't control them. They were breathing down our necks and you couldn't take a backswing for a short putt! As we played the tenth hole where we were 'all square' it was decided that we should pack it in. Someone sent for a car and we piled in and drove off to the eighteenth tee. Eleven thousand people hared after us, but we managed to drive off and Peers got a four to decide the match.

We ran into the clubhouse where we were marooned for three hours while we entertained the customers with gags and songs through a loudspeaker set. The shadows fell and suddenly everything was quiet. We exchanged 'Goodbyes' and I went home.

The next evening I was at London Airport where I was to

Happy and relaxed . . .

embark on a flight to Korea, to entertain the troops. As I walked across the tarmac it was drizzling slightly and I was halfway up the steps to board the plane when a messenger came running over to me with a telegram in his hand. It was from Bob Hope, and it said, 'BING AND I CHALLENGE YOU TO A RETURN GAME IN LOS ANGELES WITH JUST A FEW OF YOUR RELATIVES PRESENT.'

Thank you, Bing and Donald. And thank you, Bob. And thanks for the Memory.

17. 'PRO–AM' GOLF

Golf is a rapidly increasing participatory game. I believe that it stands fifth today in the ranking of sports that people indulge in, apart from just watching. Television coverage, I think, is very largely responsible for this, and driving ranges (what an excellent idea, and one that I think deserves to succeed) have also helped.

Now as far as driving ranges are concerned, I had a very unusual experience. I found that on the 'two-tiered' variety, I much preferred to play from the lower level. Somehow it was just like playing from the fairway. But on the one occasion when I had to go 'upstairs', I got a fear of 'height'. It sounds silly, and it is! But don't forget that I have an in-built vertigo, or dizziness that attacks me when I am either looking down, or looking up. I even get muzzy when I look at Tommy Cooper!

Anyway, there was this day when I arrived at the driving range on my way home from a broadcast and with my driver and my four wood in my hands, I approached the ticket office and the bloke said, 'All the downstairs berths are occupied Mr Ray, you don't mind going to the upper level?' 'Of course not,' I laughed . . . (me and my brand-new theory that was going to put twenty yards on my tee-shots!).

I climbed the stairs with the bucket of balls, and really, I was no more than fifteen feet from the ground, and I dropped the balls into the slot and prepared for my practice session. I spoke to myself aloud, and you would be surprised to learn how many golfers do!

I once said 'Hello' to an Adagio dancer who was three-handicap (and that was genuine) walking down Charing Cross Road, and his eyes were glued to the ground. 'Hello,' I shouted again and without looking up, he answered, 'Don't talk to me, Ted. I'm trying to keep my head down.' I swear that this is true. Later on he was advised by a psychiatrist to give up golf altogether. He finally did, after one evening at the Empire Sheffield when he dropped his diminutive partner into the third row of the stalls. That night he had changed his grip on her lovely form from the 'Overlapping' to the 'Interlock'.

Meanwhile (if you will excuse the passing of time), I am fifteen feet from the ground on the driving range with a brand-new theory, this being 'At the top of the backswing, feel that your grip is so light that you are almost letting go of the shaft and then through impact, increase your grip on the club.'

I get muzzy . . .

I took a practice swing and it felt really beautiful. I pressed the foot lever and down came the first ball on to the rubber tee. 'This is it,' I thought. 'The moment of truth.' I swung back easily and brought the club down. Did you ever get the feeling that you were falling from the top of the Eiffel Tower? I did! I felt that the club was pulling me into orbit, and I fell back on my right leg and the club left my hands and landed on the ground fifty feet past the ball.

'This is ridiculous,' I said to myself. 'Even with a follow-through like Gary Player's you couldn't possibly fall over the edge of the platform'—which *must* have been eight feet away. I played another shot with the four wood, but the same thing happened. As I came through the ball, I felt as if the club was going to take me with it and I just had to let go. Away went the club down the fairway, and there was nothing left to do but go down and retrieve my two clubs. All right, don't believe me, but this went on for the next hour with all these comings and goings. The chap in the ticket office must have thought that I had a very weak bladder.

I still practise at every opportunity, as does almost every theatrical performer. It's a wonderful therapy to get one's mind away from the pressure of the entertainment scene. In recent years, there have arisen many Professional–Amateur Tournaments where top-class pros are paired off with low-handicap amateurs for an additional prize for the better-ball effort. Someone had the happy idea of throwing in, for good measure, a golfer from the World of Entertainment, just to provide a few laughs, or sign some autographs, I presume.

Bing Crosby, Bob Hope, and Andy Williams are but three of the sponsors of the big-moneyed tournaments run regularly every year in the States, on these lines. In Britain, one of the earlier meetings of this kind was started by the Bowmaker Company, who for years have sponsored at Sunningdale a Pro–Am event as a sort of 'pipe-opener' for the major contests yet to come.

A few years ago I received an invitation. I really was thrilled, and replied with alacrity that I would be there to participate. There was a little cocktail party on the evening before the Competition and I was delighted beyond measure when I heard that the draw had revealed that I was 'tripled' with a low-handicapped Scottish gentleman named Donald, and the great Harry Weetman.

There was a most exciting atmosphere at Sunningdale the next day. The brightly dressed golfers on the putting green reminded one of the parade ring at Ascot, and putts being swept into the holes (with all the pressure off!) by professionals and amateurs alike, were so sweetly struck that it was, indeed, very difficult for the uninitiated to tell the difference. I felt completely relaxed, and waved to such fellow-artistes as Bruce Forsyth, Eric Sykes, and Ben Warriss as they went by.

The first tee was surrounded by some five hundred spectators. Dear old Hugh Docherty, the starter (who will ever forget his 'Quiet Please'?) was on the tee.

'Mr Charlie Drake,' he shouted. 'Calling Mr Charlie Drake. Where *is Mr Charlie Drake*?' 'He's still in MAKE-UP!' shouted Ben Warriss . . . it was that sort of day.

Finally I heard my name called. I walked nonchalantly to the first tee. On the way I met Harry Weetman. He put his hand on my shoulder. 'Remember, Ted,' he said, 'hit 'em hard, and not too often!' I still think that's wonderful advice, if you can make it work! I had never felt so calm. My most recent theory (the reverse overlap grip with the wrists hollowed and the right arm glued to the right ribs on the backswing) had been working like magic for the three previous weeks at my home course.

'Quiet please,' said Hugh. 'Mr Harry Weetman, Selsdon Park.' Harry addressed the ball. The deadly silence that greets the loneliness of the long-distance hitter. 'Harry,' I said. Weetman looked up. (He doesn't very often!) 'Pardon me, Harry,' I went on. 'What is the number on your ball?' 'It's a seven,' answered Harry. (As a matter of fact his always *is* . . . one of those little superstitions that affect the Great and the not-so-great.) 'Thanks,' I said, 'I just don't want our drives to get mixed up.'

I got the required laugh from the crowd and was quoted in the sports pages of a couple of daily papers the next morning. I had an idea that I would be, for I had observed that a few sports reporters were hanging about the first tee, and I made sure that they heard it!

Weetman got down to business and sent the ball screaming down the fairway. Mr Donald followed and hit a beautiful drive down the middle. Then Hugh Docherty said, 'Quiet please, for Mr Ted Ray, the golfing fiddler.' How the crowd laughed. 'Right,' I thought, 'I'll take the smiles off their faces.' I took a deep breath and swung the club. The ball went slicing wildly over the tall trees on the right and I holed in one through the open window of an Austin A40 that was parked in the road. When the laughter had died down and I thought the crowd had had its money's worth, I teed up another ball and this was a good shot, well short of my two partners' balls, but at least in play. As we started off followed by a fairly large crowd, a friend of mine was walking

78

behind two young lads and he heard one remark to the other, 'Did you see that first drive of Ted Ray's?'

Then his friend replied, 'Of course, but you do realize that he only did it to make us laugh!'

Would that I had that lad's confidence in my ability!

The top-class pros are wonderful to play with and never show the slightest sign of annoyance when you foozle a shot that could improve the better-ball. And I must admit that poor Harry Weetman had enough to contend with that day. I was behind more trees than the stray dog that had joined the party at the seventh!

The same thing happened when I played with the great Bobby Locke in the Bowater tournament the following year. I simply could not get a ball away from the tee. At the twelfth hole I felt I had to apologize.

'I'm very sorry, Bobby,' I said. 'My driving is shocking, and really, I'm not always as bad as this.'

'What club are you driving with, man?' asked Bobby.

I looked at him. 'Why, the driver!' I replied.

'Man,' said Bobby, 'I'm only using a three wood.' I still can't figure it out!

The single-figure handicap Irish amateur who was playing with us was also having a bad time, and with his slice, my hook, and Bobby Locke's drive on the middle of the fairway, our tee shots looked like the Prince of Wales's feathers. I felt sick as we came up the eighteenth fairway, and I'd played two and was still eighty yards short of the green, which was surrounded by spectators who were all grinning as they saw it was the fiddling comic who was about to play. Then for some wonderful reason it happened. Slowly back, head still, hands straight through to the hole, and the ball soared into the blue sky and dropped lifelessly on the green about four feet away from the hole. A burst of applause from the spectators, and a nice old gentleman came over as I walked on and said, 'Congratulations, Mr Ray, what a beautiful shot.' 'Thank you,' I answered. 'Yes,' he said, 'much better than your friend Mr Richard Murdoch, who just had a shot from the same distance.' 'Oh,' I said. 'And what did Dickie do?' 'Well,' said the nice old man. 'He hit it rather thin, skelped it over the back of the green, and rearranged all the scores on the scoreboard!'

I must say it made me feel better. Oh, by the way, I missed the putt! It wasn't my fault. Put it down to Richard Murdoch. I wasn't really concentrating. I kept thinking of some pro coming out of the clubhouse and looking up at the scoreboard wondering how his 69 could suddenly have blown up to become a 96!

Of one thing I am certain. There are influences outside our sphere that affect our deeds. The Irish call them the 'Little People' and perhaps that is the most understandable description that we can find.

Like the time when I was partnering Ian McDonald, at that time the assistant to Len Mitchell at Crews Hill Golf Club. It was a Pro–Am alliance at the Ealing Golf Club, and a highly competitive tournament. I can't recall at which hole we started, but I do know that at the seventeenth I was just short of a par five hole in two and had a golden opportunity with the stroke allowance of improving my partner's score by at least one shot.

What did I do? I'll tell you what I did! I lifted my head, I fluffed the next and I was down in six. I could have cried. Ian was sympathetic but that didn't help. I wanted to throw away my clubs. We walked silently to the last tee. The hole would be about 175 yards. Ian put his ball on the front edge of the green. I took a four wood and hit it to the back, twenty yards from the flag. Ian laid his approach putt stone dead and I knocked mine in! We won the tournament by one stroke. Ian picked up the First Pro's money and I got an electric blanket. But I'll tell you something, that blanket didn't keep me half as warm as did that twenty-yard putt!

The saddest thing I ever heard of in Pro–Am golf occurred in California. A top-class pro was paired with a wealthy amateur and, as they came to the last hole of the tournament, it really looked as though they had the whole competition 'sewn-up'. The pro was just short of the green in two, while his partner was about three yards from the hole in 'nett' 1. The amateur had three shots for the hole and the pro, no doubt allowing his partner to take the glory, told his caddie to pick up his ball.

The green was ringed by spectators, and perhaps this had an unsettling effect on the benighted player, who took a quick swipe at the putt and to everyone's horror, the poor man sent the ball skidding right past the hole and into a bunker. You can imagine the feelings of the pro golfer when his partner took four shots and still wasn't out of the sand trap. It was enough to drive a man to drink, and in fact, it actually did. He had seen 10,000 dollars fly away when almost in his grasp and he started to hit the bottle, and became a hopeless alcoholic until the day he died.

18. ECCENTRICS AND DIVOT-TAKERS
(ODDS AND SODS!)

Superstition plays a great part in the lives of most individuals. For instance there's my wife's brother. I mean, there he is! I wish he were somewhere else. I came across him the other day when I was looking through some old clothes of mine. 'Bert,' I remarked, 'tell me the truth, why don't you get a job?' He gave me that sad reproachful look, usually reserved for the losing spaniels at Crufts! 'You know me, Teddy boy,' he replied. 'I can't help it I'm superstitious. You know I can't work any week with a Friday in it.'

Please don't feel sorry for him; he has a better way of life than most of us and appears to have complete control over his conscience. I'm sorry I brought him up, as his father once said, but I wanted to get on to the point of superstition. Golfers are riddled with it.

I played with a chap in a competition the other day and he was going like a bomb, when at the tenth hole he sent his ball soaring across the trees on the right, to finish out of bounds in a field of clover, there to remain, I should imagine, for ever. 'I knew it!' he cried. 'I should never have put my left shoe on first!' Poor Harry. Also poor Arthur. He wondered why he was forever twenty-four handicap, yet placed all his faith in the rabbit's foot he carried in his back pocket. Mind you I will agree that it wouldn't be easy to carry a tiger's foot. Think of the claws in your contract! But let us paws for a moment. There I go, sorry ... I won't do it again (and I'll bet you wish I would!).

Really though, it is amazing what insignificant reasons golfers find for searching for a date with Lady Luck. Like the chap at my club who will never carry more than thirteen clubs in his bag. He claims that the permitted fourteen is unlucky for him. And that neighbour of mine I always called for in my car on Saturdays. He always kissed his wife 'Goodbye' on the day of a competition. One morning we were halfway to the course when he insisted that I take him back, because he had forgotten to peck her on the cheek. I thought it a bit much, but I humoured him. When we reached his house she had gone shopping. Sad and depressed

81

as he was we drove to the course and he won the Monthly Medal by five shots! He hasn't kissed his wife since! She has been to the Marriage Guidance Council and his home life is in shreds.

George Burns, one half of the former great American Film and TV team 'Burns and Allen', was at the London Palladium and he expressed a wish to play one of the British courses. Val Parnell, the managing director of the theatre, was obliging. He found another two players and the following morning they drove out to the pleasant Coombe Hill course in Surrey.

It was unfortunate that George Burns' golf was nothing like as crisp as his rapid-fire jokes, for he was spraying his shots all over the course and he eventually sliced a drive deep into the heart of a small forest. He was gone for some five minutes, when suddenly to the sounds of screaming and yelling he emerged with a 'bloodstained' bandage around his head, shouting, 'Run for your life . . . Red Indians on the warpath!' What he had done was to tie his handkerchief round his forehead and smother it with his wife's lipstick that he had brought with him for the purpose. Is it any wonder that Val Parnell took four putts on the next green?

There's a golfer I know who always tees up his ball about nine inches from the tee-box. Claims it makes him swing from inside to out! He and his partner needed only a six at the eighteenth to win a foursomes' final, and the poor chap missed the ball completely. His partner was left-handed. Get it! All he could do was to tap the ball into play and they lost by one shot. It isn't surprising that they have never entered as a pair again.

Little Charlie Vorzanger is an eccentric and the last things he reads at night in bed are golf books. Charlie is a gifted fiddle-player and when we met in the Gents' at the BBC a little while ago, he was limping. 'What happened?' I inquired. 'I've done my ankle in,' answered Charlie. 'I shan't be able to play for a month.' 'But how did you do it?' I asked. 'My own fault,' moaned Charlie. 'I got out of bed in the middle of the night and fell over Hogan, Snead, and Peter Thomson . . .'

At the big tournaments humble pilgrims like myself exchange these stories. True or false they are worth recounting. It was at the eighteenth hole at Wentworth that a twinkle-eyed Irishman told me, 'I'll never forget Christy O'Connor on this tee in the DAKS' tournament. He needed only a six to win it and drove his ball down the fairway. Unfortunately he cut it a bit and the ball was slicing away into the trees on the right when four young Catholic fathers, with one movement, crossed themselves and leaned over to the left. You won't believe it,' he grinned, 'but that ball changed its flight in mid-air and finished on the left-hand side of the fairway to put Christy in perfect position for his second to the green.' I gave him a quizzical look, but how could you mistrust a man with such honest blue Irish eyes?

Got out of bed . . .

The great thing is that we still go on. We always believe that tomorrow is *the* day, and that it is all going to happen.

One of the classic stories concerns the golfer who had the competition at his mercy when he shanked into a bunker at the final hole and threw away the Captain's Prize. He was inconsolable and dashing into the toilet, took a razor-blade and slashed his wrists. The place was in a panic. Doctors were called, bandages were procured, and they summoned an ambulance. His partner was more upset than anyone. He stood by the gates as they took his friend to the hospital, and he was near to tears. Suddenly the unfortunate golfer propped himself up on the stretcher, stuck his head out of the ambulance window, and shouted, 'All right, Fred, same time tomorrow?' That's what this game of golf can do to one. I'm grateful that these follies and foibles have never played any part in my own golfing life . . . touch wood!

19. 'BLIND' HOLES

A well-known amateur player from Sunningdale was enjoying a light-hearted 'four-ball' in Scotland when they came to a blind hole of some 200 yards. 'What do you think, caddie?' he asked. The Scot said, 'It's a four wood. Now if you want to fade it, play four yards to the left of yon wee post, but if you feel inclined to give it a wee bitty draw, hit it three yards to the right o' it.' 'I see,' said the golfer, 'but what about a *straight* shot?' 'With your swing,' said the caddie. 'It's not on!' The golfer, however, had the last word. 'In that case,' he said, 'go back to the clubhouse and bring me a rifle.'

In principle, I have always been against blind holes. Surely the greatest satisfaction from making a good shot is to see where the ball finishes. And imagine doing a hole-in-one? Fancy not seeing the ball actually enter the hole? The frustration of a lifetime.

At a ladies' tournament in the South of England, no less than fifteen women came into the clubhouse, and informed the card-collector that they had accomplished 'aces' at the short thirteenth. It was a hole of some 135 yards on to a basin-bowl green hidden from the tee. It transpired that an underpaid caddie with a vitriolic sense of humour had secreted himself in the bushes near to the green, and as the balls came over the hump, he dashed out and plopped them into the hole! Talk about doing a hole-in-one through an agent! I expect the bar did a roaring trade that evening.

The most remarkable blind-hole-in-one story I ever heard concerned two more than useful golfers playing almost identical shots, to a hidden green. When they arrived over the hill to play their second shots, one said, 'There's my ball two yards from the pin.'

They then searched for the other ball, and eventually found it in the hole. Obviously it was a hole-in-one. The trouble was that they then discovered that they were playing brand-new balls, both of which were stamped 'No. 3'. To this day they haven't found out which of them did the 'hole-in-one'. Isn't that terrifying? And there's a moral here. Always advise your opponent as to which ball you are playing, otherwise it could happen to you.

Mind you, it doesn't have to be a hole-in-one to cause confusion. I was playing with my friend Jack Stroud during the last war and we came to the short sixteenth. Jack played a bad one, a quick 'duck-hook' at least sixty yards left of the guide-post. During the war we had sheep grazing on the course and to my amazement, when we reached the green there was Jack's ball

Next thing he remembered . . .

lying about two feet from the pin. I strongly maintained that the ball must have been carried there by a sympathetic sheep, and for proof I showed him the teeth-marks on the ball. 'How about *that*?' I said. 'Ridiculous,' smiled Jack. 'Look at the name on the ball.' I did. It said 'Dimple Dot'. Jack proceeded to knock the putt in. I handed him the conventional shilling, which he accepted and he didn't even blush.

The third hole of the King's Course at Gleneagles has a blind second (or third) shot, depending how hard you hit 'em, and my partner, Ron Garner, was over the top of the hill in three and was playing his approach shot to the green. Now behind the green is a brass bell to which one is supposed to give a friendly tap with one's putter on leaving the green to sort of warn the following match that the green is clear. Ronnie hit his shot a bit 'thin' and his approach shot hit the bell with a resounding 'clang'. The next thing he remembered was receiving a ball from the following match right in the back of the neck. Eventually we revived him. 'Are you all right, Ron?' I asked. He rubbed his neck. 'Oh yes,' he said, 'I'm OK, but do you know what I think? Blind-holes are like left-handed golfers, they should be done away with at birth.' That's a bit harsh but I know what he meant!

20. KEEP YOUR HEAD DOWN AND NEVER CHANGE THE SIZE OF YOUR HAT

I was in the Imperial Hotel, Llandudno, and Pike, one of the head waiters, came to my table. I liked Pike. His manner and personality were perfect. Especially when he was serving the fish course. Well, naturally, he really made my day. Every day. His stories and experiences were inexhaustible.

Like the time the old man and his wife entered the dining-room one Saturday morning in June and sat down at a table for two. Pike knew that this was one of the rare occasions when they had plucked up sufficient courage to walk into a room the size of the Imperial dining-room, because the old chap was wearing his cycle clips and the old lady still had the price-tag dangling from one of her new boots. The unctuous Pike didn't turn a hair. 'Yes, sir,' he bowed. 'And what will it be?' 'Do you sell wine here?' inquired the old man. 'Oh yes!' replied the waiter. 'What kind would you like?' 'Well, this is a special occasion, see,' said the old gentleman. 'And we don't want no rubbish. This is a Golden Wedding celebration so it's got to be Champagne.' Pike smiled. 'Yes indeed, sir,' he breathed. 'I will bring you a bottle of the best.' He turned to go. The old man grabbed his arm. 'Just a moment,' he said. 'We're not mugs you know. What *voltage is it*?'

It was Pike who told me about the occasion when a so-called 'Pop Star' was entertaining his agent to lunch. A little girl of perhaps five years asked Pike if he could get the famous man's autograph, and Pike suggested that the little girl should ask him herself. She prattled over to the table and held out her autograph book and pen. 'Later,' snapped the 'Star' (if you will pardon the expression). 'Can't you see I'm eating?' I'm sure that if that little girl lived to be ninety she would never ask him again.

It is a remarkable thing, and I have said this many times, that the bigger they are the more humility they have.

It was in 1963 at Lytham St Annes that I found myself sitting on the roof of a BBC TV Outside Broadcast van and next to me was the great Arnold Palmer. Arnie hadn't had a very good OPEN and what with a heavy cold and loss of form, it was one of his more forgettable tournaments. He was doing a commentary of the final rounds when Phil Rogers and Bob Charles, (surely the greatest left-hander ever), were to tie for the title. However, there I was sitting within touching distance of Arnold Palmer and yet afraid to start a conversation. The roof of a BBC van is no place for a lesson. And then I saw the little boy. He wasn't trying to see over the heads of the crowd at the final scene, he was looking at

Palmer threw it to the kid . . .

Arnold Palmer. There was a look on his face and an expression in his eyes that I used to have for Tom Mix, the cowboy film star. He just stared. I knew how he felt. He was looking at a god. And get this. Nobody there knew about this but the kid, Arnie Palmer and me. And then something happened that made me choke. Palmer took a ball from his pocket, wrote his name on it with a ball-point pen, and threw it to the kid. He gulped and so did I. Sometimes there are scenes that don't need any words.

21. THE MISSING LINKS

Albert, Jack, and I decided that a few days on the golfing fairways of Southern England couldn't really be bad. We were all fairly free, Jack from his road-haulage commitments (strike problems), Albert a TV producer (no new shows coming up) and yours truly not very anxious to do summer cabaret with the ball running free. And so it was that we took one car with the boot full of golfing equipment and we pointed the nose of the car in a southerly direction with Hayling Island in mind.

If you have not already played the golf course at Hayling Island I commend you to so do. It is a Links course. Undulating rolling fairways, silver-sanded bunkers (what a joy it is to play out of these when your own course has natural clay and you could do with a shovel rather than a sand-wedge) and greens that are bare and fair ... this is one of the great tests of putting ... show me a player who can read fiery greens and I will show you a winner.

We were motoring on roads that were fairly traffic-free. It was a beautiful day and suddenly Albert said, 'There is a very pretty golf course near here, called Midhurst. Why don't we play a few holes there and have some lunch. After all, we are in no hurry.'

It seemed like a good idea. We decided to play nine holes and have lunch and then play another nine in the afternoon. Midhurst is pleasantly undulating and after we had been out to try the course we met a nice man in the bar who reminded me of that gentle and charming actor Mervyn Johns. It wasn't him, but he had Mervyn's nice manners and told us that he was a traveller for a firm of Italian Vermouth manufacturers.

'That's a strange coincidence,' remarked the steward, 'because that is one of the ingredients of a new cocktail that I have created. It's called "Love on the Rocks".' 'Well,' I said, 'let's try it.' 'Very well,' agreed the pleasant steward, 'but may I suggest that you have only two each, as they are pretty potent.'

I must state at this point that the steward had really invented something. After three I was asking the traveller to dance with me although there was no music, and Jack was trying to light a gherkin. After five drinks Albert had taken seven cellophane wrapped sandwiches out of a dispensing machine and refused to stop as he thought he might get the jackpot. When we had imbibed eight drinks each, we decided that it might be a good idea to go out on the course and play golf to liven us up, and we bade a lachrymose goodbye to the traveller, who was later found parked in a lay-by, in the boot of his car.

We had the course to ourselves and as we teed up we were laughing hysterically. After four attempts to make contact with the ball, Jack sliced one to mid-off and Albert hooked his over the brow of the hill. Mine went perfectly straight. Not long, but straight. I walked to my ball, which had come to rest some forty-five yards from the tee, and said to Jack, 'I am worried about Albert ... where is he?' Jack mutely pointed to the left of the fairway so I went across to find Albert. He was lying on his back, and seemed unconscious, and his golf trolley was lying on its side like a faller at the first fence of the Grand National. I really thought Albert was dead, and for a moment I was on the point of giving him the Kiss of Life, but Albert isn't really my type so I returned to Jack. He was huddled up on the grass and was also out of action. I shook him vigorously but there seemed little sign of life. I decided to go it alone. Four hours or so later, I finished the first nine holes! My score was 136 but I hadn't lost a ball.

Then I returned to the first fairway to seek my companions. There was no sign of human life, and there seemed nothing for it but to return to the clubhouse. Albert was lying on a bench in the locker-room and someone had put lighted candles at either end. I removed his clothing and washed it out in a hand-basin. I then heaved his considerable bulk with some difficulty and man-handled him to the sitting-room of the clubhouse, where the steward's wife was watching TV's 'Coronation Street', from which she refused to be disturbed.

I left the shambles of what once had been a man, and went to find Jack. He wasn't around, but I met a lone member of the club who told me that he had seen, for the first, and possibly the only time in his life, a taxi picking up two men and their equipment from the first fairway and taking them to the locker-room. Eventually I ran Jack to earth. He was sitting on a stool in the bar, asking for a remedy for a hangover. The steward suggested 'Love on the Rocks'. (Please write in for the recipe. It's not bad if you have it in bed.)

There isn't much else to tell. Jack and I heaved Albert into the back of the car ... stopped three times at pubs on the way to Southsea without any interruption from him, half carried him to his bedroom where he kissed the night-porter good night and told him he was his best friend, and Jack and I finally retired to our own rooms.

The next morning the phone rang in my room. I felt terrible. Someone had opened a trapdoor in the back of my head, and my mouth tasted as though a Portuguese family had just moved out. I picked up the phone 'Who the hell are you and what do you want?' I asked. It was Albert. Chirpy and fresh as paint. 'Come on,' he shouted. 'It's half past eight. Aren't we going to play any golf?' Strangely enough, I'm still very fond of Albert.

22. WHO SAID THAT?

If you haven't a sense of humour it's no use playing golf. What's the good of being scratch if you drop three shots in a round and can't eat your lunch? I've often said that the greatest thrill in golf is walking off the eighteenth green knowing that for the first time in your life you have broken a hundred. Everything after that is an anticlimax and you can even throw in the Open Championship.

Harry Tricker, a member of my Club, has the right idea. In trying to lower his considerable handicap, Harry decided to invest in a completely brand-new set of clubs. The other Saturday morning he appeared on the first tee with the fourteen new 'knockers', and looking at his golf bag he said to his partner, 'This reminds me of the famous words of the Duke of Wellington, gazing upon his untrained army on the eve of a famous battle: "I don't know what they'll do to the opposition, but they frighten the life out of me!"'

Inspired remarks such as this should be entered into a book for posterity. I overhead two ladies at Bush Hill Park, playing a hole which is over a lake. The player half-topped her tee shot and scuttled her ball into the water to join, no doubt, the hundreds of others that had ended their lives in a watery grave. 'Oh, what a pity, Elsie,' said her partner. 'That would have been a lovely shot if you'd hit it properly!' Work that one out. I'm still trying to.

At the very same hole on a subsequent occasion, Ron Garner was taking his tee shot. The rain was pelting down and we had already decided to walk into the clubhouse after playing the hole. Ron was garbed in the full waterproof set of jacket, trousers, and mackintosh cap. He looked at me and grinned. 'Isn't it nice, Ted,' he said, 'not to be held up by the people in front?' There wasn't much danger of that. I don't suppose there was another golfer playing within miles.

George Doonan, a great comedian in his day, was playing with me in a competition at Sudbury in Middlesex. We had started at the tenth, and George was playing the finest golf of his life. As we

93

stood on the first tee (which was, of course, *our* tenth), I felt certain that he would 'skate it' as the saying goes. George split the fairway with his drive. He addressed the ball for his second shot. He hit it a bit 'thin' and the ball shot forward, low and fast, and went right through the iron railings at the back of the green and ricocheted from gravestone to gravestone in the cemetery beyond, with the noise of a frantic xylophone. Poor George, understandably disgusted, threw his club to the ground. 'It's not fair,' he moaned. 'My wife is sitting at home enjoying herself!' I knew what he meant.

Alex Rose, the popular secretary of the Vaudeville Golfing Society, was playing at the lovely Aberdovey course in Wales. One of the short holes there is 'blind' and Alex pulled his ball to the left of the guide-post on to the sandy beach. While looking for his ball, Alex surprised a sailor and a girl who were in a rather compromising position on a sandhill. He was so astonished that he just stood there and gaped. From her recumbent position the young lady looked up over the amorous matelot's shoulder and hissed at Alex, 'How dare you. Have you no sense of decency?' I suppose it depends on your point of view.

Stanelli, who played the violin and golf rather better than I, was having a rough time during a round in Scotland. Stan was all over the place. One drive would be 'duck-hooked' and the next sliced irretrievably out of bounds. He didn't mind that so much, for he was a good loser, but what did upset him was the fact that after every shot his caddie would keep on taking out his watch and looking at it. Finally Stanelli could take it no longer. 'Don't worry about the time, caddie,' he snapped. 'I'll pay you your fee. Stop looking at your watch.' The dour caddie was unmoved. 'It's all right, sir,' he said. 'I'm in no hurry. And this is not a watch . . . it's a compass.'

Norman Evans was a great North-country comedian, but he played at golf mostly for the fresh air, I imagine. We were at a course near Birmingham and I had fixed up Norman in a four-ball, and one of the players was a fine Midlands golfer whose name was Captain Stretton-Cox. Stretton-Cox was almost one of the great amateurs and really, Norman and I had no right to be in his company on a golf course. Harold Ramsey, the Canadian Organist, made up the four, and being no fool, I chose Stretton-Cox as my partner.

On the first tee he smacked his drive about 300 yards down the fairway, and his second shot to the green was, for him, a mere formality. Norman Evans, meanwhile, was tacking from left to right and eventually he managed to get his ball on to the green. As we walked to the second tee, I pointed to my partner and I said to Norman, 'How would you like to play like him?' Norman shook his head. 'Not me,' he replied. 'You don't get enough golf.'

It was Eddy Gray, and I know I've mentioned him before in this book, who arrived on the first tee at the Royal and Ancient in St Andrews and told the caddie-master that he would like to play the famous course, but being in a hurry and having motored from Dundee, he hadn't a lot of time so could he get off right away. The kindly caddie-master approached four very senior members who were about to drive off, and he pleaded Eddy's cause. The nice old gentlemen stood aside. 'Thanks, mate,' said Eddy. 'I haven't played this ruddy game for years.' He then threw a ball into the air and took a swipe at it with a four iron. It is reported that one of the greybeards had to be assisted to the clubhouse, which is not surprising.

Once at the Braid Hills course in Edinburgh I overheard a conversation between an elderly visitor and one of the green-keepers. Apparently the old gentleman had been coming to Braid Hills during his holidays for many years and the greenkeeper and he had become great friends. As the old man walked slowly off the eighteenth green the other asked, 'And how was your golf today, Mr MacDonald?' Sadly the other shook his head and replied, 'Not verra guid, Jamie. I took seventy-three for nine holes.' 'Well, that's no' bad,' consoled Jamie. 'Why it tak's some o' them *eighteen* holes to do that!' I thought that was rather nice of Jamie.

You find a man's true character on a golf course. 'Tis said that two men were preparing to tee off one morning, when a funeral passed by. One of the golfers stopped his backswing and reverently took off his cap. The other remarked, 'Walter, that's one of the nicest gestures I have ever seen.' 'It was the least I could do,' replied Walter. 'After all, I was married to her for thirty-four years.'

My friend Big Henry lives in a house which backs on to a golf course. The strange thing is that he is not a member there, preferring to play on another course a few miles away. One day Henry showed me a letter which he had received from the secretary of the course adjacent to his home. It read thus:

Dear Sir,

Several of our members have reported that they have sliced balls out of bounds and into your garden and as they cannot cross the ditch bordering your fence I would be grateful if you would return these balls to me.

Yours, etc. etc.

'Leave this to me, Henry,' I told him. 'I will write a letter for you in reply.'

The following week I handed him this to sign:

Dear Sir,

In answer to your recent letter I would like to bring one or two facts to your notice. The unexpected arrival of golf balls in my garden has caused my wife and I considerable inconvenience. Last year three windows were broken, my dog received a cauliflower ear, and all my garden peas were prematurely shelled. Not only that but we are still using an outside toilet with a corrugated iron roof, and when my wife is occupying same, the dreadful crash of a golf ball has frightened the life out of her, and often caused her to drop her knitting.

I said only if it was raining!

96

However, I am not a spoilsport and do not intend to take further action, but I think that the least you could do is to ask your members to use decent first-grade golf balls and not the second-hand rejects and repaints that come flying over like objects from outer space.

Yours sincerely, etc.

Would you believe it? Henry has never heard another word!

But at all times give me the man with a sense of humour ... and I think the palm must go to the golfer who was preparing to take his putt on the seventeenth hole. Across the fairway came running a beautiful girl in a bridal dress. The golfer looked up and shouted, 'I said only if it was raining!' (How about that?)

23. CAN WE FIND A FOURTH?

In my travels I have met many men, and women, who wanted to play golf with me. With a name like 'Ted Ray' it's understandable, and what with mentions of it on Radio and TV, the general public has got the idea that I'm better than I am. Well, I'm not. And I hope that I shall never be accused of *thinking* I am. Like the famous film star at a Royal Film Performance. As he walked by, that fine actor Robert Beatty who was sitting next to me in the stalls during rehearsal, gave me a nudge and said, 'You know the trouble with him, Ted? He's suffering from delusions of grandeur . . . he thinks he's himself!'

Now here's a true story. Mind you, I've had to change a few names to protect the guilty, and also myself. Playing a small theatre in Wales I was approached by one of the stage-hands. 'I don't suppose you'd give us a game of golf, would you, Mr Ray, I mean me and my brother?' I combed back a stray lock of hair with my violin bow, and gave him a tolerant look. After all, I *was* the top of the bill and had my name outside the theatre in lights. It wasn't *my* fault that it said 'Red Rat' instead of 'Ted Ray' and the electrican *had* got a treble up at Newmarket, and was subsequently sacked, but that was no doing of mine.

At the time I was playing from seven handicap, and wore a pair of white plus-fours, so I repeated my tolerant look and said, 'What is your handicap?'

The man cringed. 'Well, sir,' he apologized, 'I'm only five.' There was a moment's silence and then I inquired, 'And what handicap does your brother have?' 'Oh, he's two,' came the answer.

Now I was interested. The chap must have been lying, or else he didn't know what the term 'Handicap' meant. Perhaps he thought he received five shots on every hole. I had to find out. 'Can we get a fourth?' I asked. 'Oh yes,' he replied. 'We'll get little Billy as your partner. You'll like little Billy and he thinks the world of you.'

Now I knew I shouldn't have asked but I felt compelled to. 'And what's Little Billy's handicap?' 'Scratch,' came the answer, and at that moment the orchestra struck up my opening music and I was 'On'. I wasn't very funny that night. For some reason or other I couldn't concentrate and later found that I had cracked the same joke twice.

Next morning I drove out to the course and the chap who had approached me and whose name, believe it or not, was Brynwyd, was waiting on the first tee. He had another fellow with him, and he looked like a gorilla wearing a man's suit, which was definitely 'off the peg'. 'Oh, Mr Ray,' said the stage-hand, 'this is my brother Evan.' Evan removed his cap and curtsied. 'It's a great honour, sir,' he said. I looked around. 'Where's Little Billy?' I asked. Brynwyd looked around. 'Why, here he comes now ... you'll like little Billy.'

Approaching us was a young man of perhaps twenty-five. He walked with flat feet, like a steward on an ocean-going liner, whose arches had fallen through continuous contact with the carpets, and Little Billy was about three stone overweight. His trousers were nicely creased ... all over, and he wore a white shirt and a flat cap, from beneath which tufts of black hair sprouted. But he had a beautiful smile and lovely eyes. 'Hello, Billy,' I said, extending my hand. He held it with a gentle grip, and I remember thinking to myself, 'Scratch? Who is kidding *who*?' Brynwyd said, 'It's a lovely day, Mr Ray, and there aren't too many people on the course, so we should have a leisurely round.' 'Not *too* leisurely,' I thought. There was a tall cool blonde in the hotel and she had been giving me that interesting look over her prawn cocktail, and the theatre didn't have a matinee that afternoon, so I said, 'Well, lads, let's see who's on form today.'

Brynwyd and Evan gave Billy and me the honour and I teed up. The first hole was a short one, say 150 yards. I took a slow meaningful swing and put my ball pin-high, unfortunately in a deep bunker. Little Billy laid his tee-shot stiff by the flag and the two was a mere formality. Brynwyd and the gorilla each had threes, without apparent difficulty, and we proceeded to the second tee. Well, I won't bore you with all the details, but Little Billy and I won on the last green. The opposition had used all their shots, they had both broken seventy (gross), and I had been 'in' twice. The great thing was that I had enjoyed every moment of it. They were such nice fellows, and no one had ever mentioned a money bet. They just loved it and were so thrilled to think that I had agreed to play with them, that it was very touching. And Little Billy! If I live to be a hundred I shall never forget the poetry of motion of that wondrous swing, and I've seen most of the Greats.

I often think of Little Billy and the brothers. Especially when I think of two other brothers who both play from false handicaps and never play unless it's for big money. And sometimes when I have a restless night I dream of bringing Little Billy along and telling the opposition that he is eighteen handicap, and laying on a sizeable stake. I would of course mark Billy's card, and tell him to play bad golf until the opposition was four up and then say quietly, 'OK, Bill, turn it on,' and he would, to order, with that perfect swing, and we would 'clean up' and double the stakes on the 'bye'. And then it's just about that time that I wake up and realize that it's just a dream. Do you know why? Little Billy wouldn't do it. He's not that kind of a chap.

24. WHO SAYS LIGHTNING NEVER STRIKES TWICE?

One of the nicest fellows I ever met was a bloke called Jack Rollings. We were in a revue together and Rollings was a dancer, and a very good one, almost in the Fred Astaire/Gene Kelly class. His feet looked like they'd had a college education, but unfortunately he could do nothing with his hands. Well, anyway, not on a golf course. If you were smart, directly he teed up a ball you'd look for a place to hide. He is the only man I have ever played with who could put a ball out of bounds backwards! Rollings was very nervous. He wasn't exactly mad about Show Business, but he told me he only took it up because he was too nervous to steal. But the lad was game, and he would play from morning till night, his hands covered in blisters, and his golf bag devoid of balls, and still grin and say, 'Ted, I did enjoy that!' He must have been a golfing masochist.

When players with much greater ability were turning over in bed on a rainy morning, Rollings would be waiting at the stage door of the theatre, ready to go out to the golf course and hack his way around.

I shall never forget our week in Bristol. I'd popped down to see if there were any letters and there was Jack with that lovely permanent grin on his face and he said, 'I'm glad you've come, I thought I'd have to go round on my own.' I looked at him. 'What the hell are you talking about?' I asked. 'Have you seen the weather?' It really was a terrible day, and the rain was tearing down the gutters in torrents. 'Oh, it'll clear up,' said Rollings cheerfully.

I should have known better, of course, but the idiot talked me into it. We drove to the Long Ashton golf course. We signed the visitors' book, and the steward hardly gave us a look. I suppose he'd got used to the half-wits who play in any old weather, and we adjourned to the locker-room to change. Then Jack discovered that he'd forgotten to bring his golf shoes. Of course, I was delighted after having been talked into playing golf on a day so appalling as this. 'Look,' I said. 'There must be three hundred pairs of shoes here and I'm sure no one would mind if you borrowed a pair.' 'Ah, but you see,' protested Rollings, 'I have very small feet,' and this was true. Believe me, if he had been trying on the crystal slipper, he would have beaten Cinderella to the Ball. 'Well, that's your only chance,' I advised, secretly hoping that he wouldn't find any, and that we could go back to the City and have a 'livener'. (For the uninitiated that's the first drink of the day, and it's the best one.)

He started rooting around and suddenly shouted, 'I've found a pair.' They were made of rubber and were very dusty. In one of them was a dead matchstick, some cobwebs and a tram ticket, and I said, 'Well, all right, you'll be safe in borrowing those, so let's go out and get on with it.'

I didn't see much of Jack for the first four holes. Except on the tees, that is. He was slicing, hooking, shanking; you name it, and he was doing it. Meanwhile the rain had steadily increased and the holes were filling up with water. When you sank a putt the ball slowly disappeared, like a wrecked ship going down into the depths, and I said, 'Come on, Jack, enough is enough.' The fool wanted to play on, but I was adamant.

We sloshed our way back to the clubhouse and met three men who were standing outside the door. Rollings smiled. 'Terrible morning, isn't it?' he said. One of them looked down and said, 'Where did you get those?' Rollings blushed. 'Get what?' he stammered. The other pointed. 'Those shoes,' he said. 'You're wearing my shoes.' 'Oh,' said Rollings. 'I don't think so.' The man snorted. 'Well, I bloody well *know so* . . . *get* them off and put 'em back where you found them.' Rollings was trembling, and I really felt sorry for him.

We changed hurriedly and drove back to Bristol as fast as we could. 'Can you beat it?' said Jack. 'Three hundred pairs of shoes and I take size five and a half and they had to be his. The odds against that must have been as great as winning a football pool.'

A fortnight later Jack Rollings got nine draws in one column and won £47,000. He stayed with the show for another month and then gave in his notice. I never saw him again.

Another friend of mine who had cause to be embarrassed was named Jack Hobbs. No, he didn't play cricket and his golf was only fair, but he was a nice character and a cheerful companion. He received an invitation to play at Wentworth in a Society meeting. It was a really beautiful day in May and there is no more pleasant place to be than Wentworth when the sun is shining and

Jack almost felt like breaking into song as he prepared to take his first drive.

For those unfortunates who have not yet played the BURMA ROAD, as they call the West Course, let me explain that the road leading from the main road to the clubhouse runs directly in front of the first tee and, when a big pro tournament is being played, a man with a rope holds back the incoming cars until the players have driven off. On ordinary days the players and car drivers are expected to exercise care. Jack was unaware of this, and put everything into his drive at the very moment that a gleaming limousine appeared from round the bend. There was a terrifying crack like the sound of a pistol shot as the ball met the door panel. Naturally the car stopped and the driver got out.

Jack went forward and stammered, 'I really am terribly sorry, but I didn't see you coming. Why didn't you sound your horn?' The other looked fit to explode. 'Sound my horn?' he snorted. 'I've been a member here for twenty years and I've never *had* to sound my horn, because people here take care to make sure that it's all clear before they drive. I've never seen you before, who the hell are you?' 'Jack Hobbs,' came the reply, and Jack told me that he really thought the fellow was going to strike him. 'Honestly, it really *is* Jack Hobbs,' and the other glared. 'Another thing,' he growled. 'It wouldn't be so bad if this was an old car, but I only got it this morning, just look what you've done.' It really was a terrible dent, as if someone had done it with a heavy mallet. Jack offered to pay, but the other refused to accept any money, and after a few more words, drove the car in the direction of the car-park.

Naturally enough, the incident upset poor Jack and his golf went to pieces for the first few holes, but after a while he settled down and began to improve. On the back nine he was actually enjoying himself and hit a beautiful drive straight down the fairway. He reckoned he only needed a seven iron to reach the green and he prepared to play the shot. Unfortunately right at the top of his backswing, he heard some shouting and this caused him to lift his head and top the ball, which ran about ten yards. From across the fairway came a man, who didn't appear to be too happy because his face had gone purple and he was shaking his fist. As he approached, Jack's heart fell. 'Now look here,' he said, 'I've apologized for denting your car, and even offered to pay, so why don't you forget it?' 'It's got nothing to do with that,' yelled the man. 'You've just played my ball.' By a coincidence they were both using balls with the same number. Jack walked forward, and picking up the ball he handed it to the other man. He looked at it and silently stretched out his arm for Jack to see. The ball was almost severed. 'You're a menace,' breathed the victim of Jack's mistake. 'You should be chained up, you should never be allowed to play on any course again, and if you joined this club, I would resign.' And with that he strode away.

Jack's day was ruined, of course. No man living could have expected to play anything like good golf at such a moment. It was a merciful release when the round was over, and he reached the haven of the nineteenth hole. Jack's host told him to forget it, and that it could happen to anyone. What with this and the pleasant effect of a scotch and soda, Jack finally began to cheer up. About half an hour later, in walked the man with the purple face, which wasn't purple by now, but he gave Jack a glare that wouldn't have disgraced a basilisk, as he approached the bar.

Jack's friend grabbed his arm. 'Now come on, Benson,' he said softly. 'You must meet my friend. Why he's one of the best and you've no idea how unhappy he has been all morning. These things happen you know, and you must realize that he wouldn't do them on purpose.'

Benson was silent for a moment and then he put out his hand which poor Jack grabbed gratefully. 'Thanks, Mr Benson,' he gasped. 'Once again please accept my profound apologies. Let me buy you a drink?' 'Oh, that isn't necessary,' said the other. 'Oh, but it *is*,' pleaded Jack. The mollified Benson said he'd have a scotch and soda. 'Yes, a *large* one,' beamed Jack happily, and he ordered it and handed it over to Benson. Jack picked up the soda siphon and said, 'Say when.' Disaster followed. Poor Jack was so excited that he pressed too hard and the scotch and soda shot up and splashed all over Benson's shirt front!

I looked at Hobbs. 'And what did he say?' I inquired. 'I don't know,' replied Jack. 'I ran out of the bar, grabbed my clubs and holdall, and drove home without changing.' Jack Hobbs understood why I laughed, because it hadn't happened to me, and time had dimmed the misery and pain he had experienced that May morning. 'Have you played Wentworth since?' I asked him. He gave me a grin. 'Oh yes,' he said. 'But I always start at the second!'

25. FACE TO FACE

If my golfing experiences have taught me one lesson above all others it is to come to terms with myself. That splendid writer on golf, Kenneth Wilson, said that every golfer should have a large card pinned to the inside of his locker saying 'Golfer— Know your limitations'. I'll certainly go along with this and what wonderful advice it is. What's the use of driving a ball across a ditch 200 yards away if it only lands 10 yards over the other side, if the second shot is 250 yards from the green? What's the point in taking the unnecessary risk? In any case we are not all gifted with the ability to produce prodigious length, and a six-inch putt counts just as much as a 300-yard drive. If the handicapping committee, in its generosity and wisdom, gives one a few shots, why throw them away? In any case in every profession a 'pro' is a 'pro', so don't make the mistake of trying to match him shot for shot.

A musician of my acquaintance arrived at Crews Hill one day and challenged Charles Whitcombe to a game. Charles was generous and offered to play off 'Plus-four' so the trumpet player got the full allowance. Charlie gave him the honour and the amateur drove a good shot some 230 yards down the centre of the fairway. Whitcombe pulled his drive a little and it buried itself in a bush. As he pulled the ball out and dropped it over his shoulder, his opponent said, 'What are we playing for, Charles, shall we say a quid?' 'Very well, sir,' replied Charlie quietly, and proceeded to lay the ball 'stiff' alongside the hole with a six iron. Somewhat shattered, his opponent 'thinned' a four iron into an impossible lie over the green and lost the hole. As they left the green he turned to Whitcombe and said, 'On second thoughts I think we'll make the bet five bob.' 'Yes, sir,' smiled Charles. 'I think that might be better.'

In any case the musician should have known better than to tangle with a man like Charles Whitcombe, who once went round the Crews Hill Course in fifty-nine gross without even a 'two' or a 'five' on his card, and remember the par of the course was seventy-two! And really, if one can't laugh at one's own mistakes one has no right to play the game.

They say that the Hendon Golf Club has exactly 365 bunkers, one for every day of the year. I played there in a Society meeting a few years ago and in the morning round I think that I must have found every one of them. My caddie had a marvellous sense of humour. When, after lunch I appeared on the first tee, I saw that he had added a strange implement to my clubs. It was a child's seaside sand-shovel hanging from which was a calendar. I laughed so much that I forgot all my mid-morning misery. It took off all the pressure and we had quite a pleasant round.

I was contending a final with a fellow-sufferer, and it was one of those days that they advertise in the holiday magazines and that we experience so rarely here in Britain. The sun was warm, a light breeze was sifting behind my right ear, and the premature butterflies were winging their gossamer ways to their early pre-demise. It was a day that made one feel good to be alive. 'Isn't it a glorious day, Harold,' I remarked as we stood on the tee of the short tenth. 'Yes, it is,' growled Harold. 'And you're three up!'

But golfers are very respectful and aware of the feelings of others. I once took a walk with my wife Sybil and we were traversing a public footpath that bisects the Crews Hill course. Two of our longer-handicapped members were about to drive off. Knowing the standard of their play, I reckoned that there was only a fifty-fifty chance of their hitting the ball in 'one'. I also knew that they would be very conscious of our presence. At that particular moment a man only wants to be with his opponent, his clubs, and his God, in reverse order. I squeezed Sybil's arm. 'Don't look, dear,' I murmured. 'Why not?' she whispered. 'What are they going to do?'

How about the two chaps who went to the classy golf club for a friendly round and after signing the visitors' book and ordering lunch, made their way to the first tee and prepared to play. They stood there, nonplussed, for fifteen minutes or so when the secretary opened the window of his office and said, 'Gentlemen, you have signed the book and ordered lunch, why don't you drive off?' One of the players pointed to the tee. There was a brand-new ball, in all it's pristine whiteness, resting on a peg-tee and reflecting the light of the springtime sun. 'I'm afraid there is someone ahead of us,' he shouted. 'We'll have to wait for him.' 'Oh, don't worry about that,' said the secretary. 'That's Colonel Parker's ball, HE OFTEN COMES DOWN AND TAKES A SWIPE AT IT!'

It may be funny to you but it was deadly serious to Colonel

Parker. We have only two Life members at our club. One plays four holes all by himself every morning, then sits under a tree with the *Financial Times*, and eats cheese sandwiches. He must be a millionaire. It is said that he was the man who invented cabinet towels so that he wouldn't have to tip the lavatory attendant. His handicap is, and always was, twenty-four.

The other week at the end of a committee meeting, someone remarked, 'What about old Purvis?' 'Well, what about him?' asked the chairman. The other remarked, 'He has been twenty-four handicap all his life, don't you think it would be a good idea if we made him twenty-two ... it would make his life.' With a chuckle the rest of the committee agreed.

On the following Saturday old Purvis walked into the Club and gave a cursory glance at the list showing the recent deliberations of the handicapping committee. His eyes popped out like organ stops. 'Twenty-two!' he exclaimed. After all these years!

He put on his old rubber golf shoes with new hope and made his way to the first tee where the other three old crocks were waiting for him. Three and a half hours later he walked off the eighteenth green. The secretary espied him on his way to the clubhouse. Throwing open his window he shouted, 'How was it, Mr Purvis, how was it?' Purvis gave him a baleful glance. 'How was it?' he cried. 'I played like a ruddy twenty-four handicap golfer.'

I make no apology for bringing Eddy Gray into the limelight again, because there are so many unbelievably true stories about him. He had just finished a round at New Malden in Surrey and was indulging in a 'snifter' at the nineteenth and chatting with Alex Laidlaw the professional. The conversation developed into a friendly argument and Laidlaw finally said, 'Oh, come off it, Eddy, I could beat you with only a putter.' Eddy gave him that blank stare. 'All right,' he said. 'We'll play one hole, the first. You use the putter and I'll use any clubs I like.' 'Done,' said Alex. 'And I'll take you on for a pound.' Eddy agreed, and off they went to the first tee. Never tangle with a pro. Eddy hit a fair drive down the middle. Laidlaw, with a putter (which to a pro is practically a Number 1 iron) put the ball thirty yards past Eddy's shot and Eddy put his second shot on the green, but so did Alex Laidlaw. The only difference was that the pro got a three to Eddy's four.

They walked back to the bar and after half an hour or so, Eddy said, 'All right, mate, but I bet you couldn't do it again.' 'Let's find out,' said Laidlaw, and out they went once more where, believe it or not, exactly the same thing happened. Eddy gave up, and who wouldn't? Poor Alex Laidlaw, a young man of whom so much was expected in the world of golf. He went off to war and never came back.

I always find it strange to play with a Southpaw golfer, a man who stands the 'wrong way round'. The way it applies in golf is usually that he has his left hand below his right on the shaft of the club, and he stands with his back to the tee-box. You don't get much conversation during a round with a 'southpaw' unless he slices and you hook. Or vice versa. Or, of course, if you both hit 'em straight, but who does?

One of the most amusing left-handers I ever had the good fortune to play with is Ben Warriss who is now the owner of a lovely roadhouse restaurant at Colerne in Wiltshire. You can get a splendid meal there, and Ben has adapted himself to the business of looking after the comforts of his patrons with enthusiasm and success. He even puts the knives and forks down the right way round when he lays the tables. Well, it can't be easy for a 'southpaw'.

Like most of us Ben has had little patience with his own mistakes and I have actually seen him unwrapping a brand-new ball before its predecessor had hit the road over the out-of-bounds fence on the right.

'The bloke who designed this course must have been drunk,' snapped Ben. 'And they've *all* got something against left-handers.'

I would meet him around the provinces when we were touring with Revues and once I followed him into the Palace, Manchester. I'd been having a little trouble with my six iron and one evening I was getting dressed for the Finale of the show and decided to take a practice swing in front of the mirror. I took the club back and there came a terrible crash as I destroyed the overhead chandelier. Now there used to be a notice on the walls of the theatres stating that artistes had to make good any damage for which they were responsible, and having duly sent for the manager, my mind was working in sheer desperation to think of an alibi before I showed him what I had done. I quickly told my dresser and, when Willie Taylor came in I was all prepared. 'It's like this, Willie,' I explained. 'I had put on my evening dress shirt and tie and trousers and was just getting into my coat when

108

foolishly I was still holding my silver-topped ebony stick ... my arm went up in the air and that was that.'

Willie sighed. 'Oh well, it can't be helped I suppose, but only last week the same thing happened when Ben Warriss broke the chandelier while opening a bottle of champagne.'

About a month later I met Ben in the Club. 'Say, Ben,' I said, 'did you play the Palace, Manchester, a few weeks ago and break a chandelier in the dressing-room with a champagne cork?' 'Yes, Ted,' replied Ben ... 'that's right.' 'Ben,' I asked. 'Which club did you use?' He looked me straight in the eye. 'Why, a six iron,' he grinned. 'What else?'

26. THE STAG PARTY

Every year in November on a certain Sunday evening, several men in dinner jackets may be seen making their way down Park Lane in London's West End to foregather for an Annual Dinner which has been going on for over forty years. It is comparatively simple to sort out the guests from the members. The former nearly all wear clean collars, whereas, on close inspection, the collars of the members have thin pink edges, caused by wear the previous evening at some TV show, cabaret performance or hot-pot supper in a pub. The pink edge is really theatrical make-up, and if one of these worthies is a dancer, his patent-leather shoes will probably have metal taps on the soles.

Now the guests by far outnumber the members, the latter being the descendants and successors of a small band of touring theatrical performers who got together years ago and decided to call themselves the 'Vaudeville Golfing Society'. It wasn't long before most of them began to wear 'Plus-fours', some of which were of such a length and voluminous width that they wouldn't have looked out of place on members of the French Foreign Legion.

The membership grew as Show Business people came to realize that they could get just as round-shouldered swinging a golf club as by pushing open pub doors, and the air was purer as well, and soon they were able to pay a subscription to become affiliated to golf clubs all over the country. I have recorded elsewhere in this book how I came to join this brave and enthusiastic band, and I never had cause to regret it. To mix with such famous people as Will Fyffe, Billy Merson, and Bud Flanagan was a position of exaltation beyond my powers of comprehension.

One day I was playing golf with the secretary who informed me that there was an Annual Stag Party and would I care to purchase a ticket. Would I? You bet I would, even if this meant that I had to buy a dinner jacket and all the rest of the outfit. This presented some difficulty, as clothes were very expensive and I certainly couldn't afford a *new* one.

Then providentially came the solution. I was on a bill at a

music hall in Barnsley and sharing a dressing-room with a turn who called himself Alf Hartigan. His real name was Bert Parker, and he was half of a double act called Parker and Bray. Parker told me he was trying out a single act for a comic who was afraid to go on and do it himself. I asked what had happened to Bray and Parker told me that he had died a fortnight previously. Now many performers 'die' (as it is known in the profession when the audiences are unsympathetic, or on some occasions antagonistic) but apparently this time it was the real thing. Harry Bray had heard the voice of the Number One 'Call Boy' and passed on to bigger and better theatres in the sky. It transpired that Bray's wife had deserted him some years before and left for Australia with a one-armed flute-player, and Parker was left with (if you'll pardon the expression) the 'effects' of the deceased. During our conversation Parker mentioned that Bray had left a dinner jacket suit in his travelling trunk and at once I pricked up my ears. 'How much?' I asked. Parker replied, 'Oh, I couldn't charge you for that.' 'Oh, come on, Bert,' I said. 'I must give you something . . . how much?' 'Very well,' sighed Parker. 'Three quid.' Now for a man who couldn't charge me anything, three quid in those days was a considerable sum, but I needed that suit. 'Done,' I said. We shook hands. I was lucky to get my signet ring back. Parker was a hard man.

Now I don't suppose that many of you have been present at the opening of a touring artiste's cabin trunk. It is rather like the legendary Pandora's Box, and all that remained of the late Harry Bray's possessions were Hope and a dinner jacket suit. 'Poor Harry,' said Parker sadly. 'He had a heart as big as himself.' Well, all I can say is that it must have been some heart because when I tried on the trousers and pulled them up, I blindfolded myself. I looked like a midget going down in a lift. The jacket also engulfed me. 'Plenty of room,' beamed Parker. 'Are you kidding?' I asked. 'Get three more in here and we can play bridge.' Bert was equal to the occasion. 'We'll get Morry,' he soothed.

I was to discover that Morry Getz, who was also appearing on the programme, would be my salvation. Morry did an act known as Regurgitation. In other words, he swallowed things and immediately brought them up again. His ultimate ambition was to swallow an electric globe and a pocket watch so that a member of the audience could tell the time by his navel. This frequently brought on stomach trouble and he had to have medical attention. The usual treatment was an emetic, but even then he couldn't keep it down.

Now I knew all about this part of Morry's life, but what I wasn't aware of was the fact that he carried around in his basket a portable sewing machine, and this was why Parker had taken me to his dressing-room. Morry gave me an estimate. 'Ten bob,' he said. 'And you'll think it came from Savile Row.' More expense. I began to think that it would have been cheaper to go to a second-hand clothes shop or an undertaker's. There must have been someone of my size lying there who had no further use for his dinner jacket. However, I was in far too deep now to go back, so I told Morry to get on with it, and make no mistake, the fellow was good. He cut and carved and stripped and sewed, and when he'd finished I looked in the mirror and nodded my approval. Morry was also delighted. He had enough cloth left over to make an evening dress suit for a penguin that was working in an act presented by the Great Aquarius who was closing the first half of the show.

It was a very nervous young comic who presented his ticket at the hotel on the night of the Dinner. You know how it is when for the first time you walk into a room where there's a large gathering. Eventually I saw a fellow with whom I had worked in a revue and he motioned me over. Bert Rogers was standing with two or three other men and they all held cocktail glasses. I shook hands with Bert and he motioned to the chap on his left. 'Ted, my boy,' said Bert cheerfully. 'This is the Marquess of Queensberry.' 'I know,' I replied. 'And I'm Lord Mountbatten.' He wasn't going to get away with that! 'You fool,' hissed Bert. 'It *is* the Marquess!'

I didn't know where to look and I was relieved when the toastmaster called us in to dinner. I was looking forward to this and when I read the menu I was ready to do full justice to it. The waiter had just served the oysters when the secretary of the Society came over and whispered in my ear. 'Bert Grant hasn't turned up,' he informed me. 'He's fixed a Sunday concert in Luton and can't make it. Would you be a sport and propose the toast to the Guests?' Then he walked away.

The fork in my hand trembled and the oyster slipped down my shirt front to parts unknown. My appetite had disappeared. There is a classic story of a Christian in the Colosseum in Rome being sacrificed to a hungry lion when the poor benighted man walked across to the beast and whispered into its ear. The lion's tail dropped between its legs and it skulked out of the arena. The Emperor Nero sent for the Christian and said, 'I will pardon you if you will tell me what you said to the lion.' The man replied simply, 'All I said was, "Don't forget you will be expected to say a few words after dinner."'

A bit upset for a moment...

Believe me I knew how that lion felt. What was I going to say? I had no knowledge of the visitors' names or who were present. In desperation I decided to resort to my act. The old gags. What I always called the 'Tried and Trusted'. Two or three speakers arose and made their speeches. They were good, they were *very* good and had all obviously made great preparation. I felt awful. I had eaten nothing, and through some sort of fog I heard my name called. I rose and heard a voice which sounded vaguely like my own saying, 'It gives me great pleasure ...' what a mockery

113

that was. I bumbled and mumbled through my time-honoured jokes and heard a few titters. I gained strength and after ten minutes or so I sat down to a smattering of applause. After all it hadn't been too bad. Then the toastmaster hammered his gavel and said, 'The reply from the Guest of Honour, the Marquess of Queensberry,' and that distinguished gentleman rose and proceeded to speak quite brilliantly. After a minute or so I realized that he was taking me apart and I suddenly got the message that I hadn't even mentioned his name. Finally he said, 'Oh, on behalf of the guests I thank you for this hearty welcome, and in case you do not know, I hold the title of the Marquess of Queensberry, and we do have rules.' He then looked me straight in the eye and sat down. I was a bit upset for a moment, but later on I was grateful to him. He had given me my first lesson in making a speech. That was years ago, of course, and since then I can modestly say that I have become one of the best after-dinner speakers in the country. In the *town*, nothing, but in the country not bad at all!

The practical jokes that are perpetrated at the Annual Dinner of the VGS are almost unbelievable. On one occasion a guest rose to propose the health of the Society and for at least ten minutes he spoke about the wanton destruction of fish in Lough Neagh. 'How aircraft,' he protested, 'in bombing practice, can wantonly destroy that king of fish, the noble salmon, is beyond my comprehension.' The members of the Society were becoming restless and understandably so. After all they had paid good money to hear witty speeches about golf. The murmur was becoming what we call in the profession, a 'rhubarb'. Try saying the word rhubarb softly over and over again and you will get the idea. Eventually the secretary had a word with the toastmaster and that worthy approached the speaker and informed him: 'Sir, this is the Vaudeville Golfing Society,' whereupon the orator, in a voice just loud enough to be heard by the assembled multitude, replied, 'Oh, is this not the annual meeting of the Royal Piscatorial Society?' only to receive a sad shake of the head from the toastmaster. 'Good heavens,' gasped the 'guest', 'I'm at the wrong bloody dinner!' He then walked out of the room and never returned.

On another occasion the astonished diners witnessed a stand-up fight between two 'waiters' who threw plates, bread rolls, cups, saucers, and glasses at each other before being ejected from the room by two policemen who were called in. The four of them were, it transpired, unemployed acrobats and tumblers who were well paid for the job.

And can you imagine a woman in nightdress, dressing-gown, and hair curlers dragging out of the room her 'husband' because he was 'always out with his drunken friends getting half-cut'. I tell you, it was hilarious.

One night we had as guests of honour three dusky princes from Jordan, in turbans and silken robes, and they seemed to enjoy themselves as much as anybody present. Then dear old Bud Flanagan announced that their Highnesses were leaving, whereupon the whole room stood to attention while the band played a seemingly interminable National Anthem of their country, but as the three princes reached the stage at the end of the room, they hitched up their robes and went into a three-handed dance routine that wouldn't have disgraced a coloured dancing act, for in fact, that is what they were!

During one of the years of my own captaincy, the toastmaster announced that I would say Grace, which I proceeded to do, but mumbling unintelligibly into the table microphone. One of the company shouted, 'I can't hear you!' 'Shut up,' I replied, 'I'm not talking to you.' Irreverent? I don't really think so.

If there is one night I shall never forget, it is the occasion when one of our members, doubtless meaning well, invited as his guest the Bishop of Perth, Western Australia. Unfortunately, the reverend gentleman, though charming and affable, cast rather a damp blanket over the proceedings which were usually, in fact *always*, uninhibited, and the various speakers found themselves tongue-tied as they had to cut out joke after carefully rehearsed joke in deference to the cloth and gaiters.

It was a gloomy evening. Finally the bishop rose to reply to the toast of 'The Guests'. He started quietly enough, but gradually warmed to his subject and proceeded to describe what he thought of the Vaudeville Golfing Society and its members. It was terrific. Even the organists in his own particular diocese could never have pulled out more stops. Once again the assembly realized that they had fallen for the 'three card-trick' when it was disclosed that he was an out-of-work character who needed the money. The 'Bishop' sat down to a roar of applause, beaming at his congregation, and sitting there with a king-sized cigar in one hand and a large scotch in the other. From that moment on, the fun and frolic waxed fast and furious.

27. 'SHOW-BIZ' GOLF

I make no apologies for this being the longest chapter in this book. Show Business has been my life. It almost didn't happen. Once when my mother read out the 'Riot Act', and demanded that I try to find a 'decent' job, I was actually a finalist of two for a job as a haberdasher's assistant, at the then highly paid wage of £2 10s. 0d. per week. I said a silent 'Thank you' to the 'One upstairs' when I failed to get the position by a whisker. Actually it was on a technicality. The interviewer, who suffered from dyspepsia and kept giving repeat performances through his moustache, asked me this question. 'What would you say to a man who complained that the sleeves of his shirt were always becoming soiled?' Quickly I answered, 'Sell him a pair of celluloid cuffs and a rubber.' It transpired that this was not the answer the examiner was looking for. The answer, it appeared, was 'a pair of armbands'. Apparently these haberdashers don't seem to care if you get a pair of gravy-stained wrists.

Luckily, my mama didn't have to wait too long, and within a few days replies from some of the letters I had written to agents asking for a chance to 'be seen' began to roll in. I picked out a date for London, as I thought that there would be more opportunity there. I prospered, and within a year I knew that Show Business would be kind to me, and that this would be my life. I have already explained in Chapter 1 of this book how I first took up the game and shall now recount the experiences I have had with some of my fellow-artistes on the golf course and also in the dressing-rooms of the music halls. (Don't start drooling, I'm only talking about the men!)

In an earlier chapter I told how I came to take up golf, and there is no doubt that it was the wisest thing I ever did. When I came into Show Business, none of the artistes rose before noon. They would then go down to the stage door of the theatre, hoping to find there a contract from some agent or other and then, providing they had the necessary cash, would saunter to the local 'theatrical house of call' (can you beat that?) and talk 'shop' among themselves, or tell stories, to entertain some of the local tradesmen, who would kindly ply them with drink until closing time. Somewhat muzzily they would then return to the 'digs', to be greeted with a mouthful of vituperation (how about *that* word? . . . those days at the Liverpool Collegiate School weren't wasted) from the poor old landlady who had cooked the meal more or less to perfection for 1 pm. 'Don't worry, Ma,' the 'pro' would say airily, 'I'm sure it will be delicious.' After consuming the meal, and not really knowing whether it was steak and kidney pie or Apple Charlotte, nor caring, if the truth be known, our thespian would take off his jacket, loosen his braces, and sink on to the bed to snore it off before the poor landlady would bring him a strong cup of tea at 5 pm and then he would go off to the theatre, with a bit of a headache, which disappeared miraculously as soon as he had slapped the make-up on his face and put on his stage clothes.

It was a pointless existence for most of them, and work was so hard to come by and engagements so sporadic, that very few retired rich or independent. Some would take over the manager-ships of pubs, when their voices or memories failed, and if they could get a pub near to a music hall they would be in their seventh heaven, greeting friends old and new and living once again their triumphs (but seldom their failures!).

So I think I was fortunate to have taken up golf so early in my theatrical career, as I became so keen that I would ask the aston-ished landlady if she would call me at 8 am so that I could get away comfortably from the first tee. In those early days I played mostly on my own, as I didn't think myself fit to give anyone else a game. I was very happy however, thrashing and slashing the ball around, and I am certain that I must have visited parts of the course that the local members had never seen. Of course this beginning is quite wrong, and if I had my time over again, I would go immediately to a professional and learn the real way to play and then perhaps I wouldn't have the ingrained faults that are part of my swing. The professional golfer likes to catch 'em young. Children are born mimics, and will immediately do as they are told. How different from trying to get some plump housewife to pivot a little more, or asking an old retired major to cock his wrists, when he can't even cock a snook! No, it's far better to learn properly when one is young.

I heard of a lady who took her little boy to a professional and said, 'I thought it would be best to bring him to you now, so that he will be a really fine player when he grows up.' 'Great,' replied the pro. 'How old is he?' 'Oh, he's only nine,' beamed Mama.

'What a pity,' said the pro. 'Four years wasted.'

In spite of my ignorance, however, the time came when I

Four years wasted . . .

could actually hit a ball in one, and I began to keep my scores assiduously and I never cheated. Well, is it worth it? You are only kidding yourself. It was some time before I broke a hundred, and what a day that was for me. I couldn't have felt better if I had won the Open. I dashed back to my digs and proudly showed the card to the landlady, bless her. She didn't understand a word, but she tried to look suitably impressed. And I'll tell you something about breaking a hundred at golf. Statistics have proved that out of all the golfers who play, only $16\frac{2}{3}$ per cent ever break one hundred. Think of that next time you do a ninety-nine and are ready to jump off a cliff!

I was now ready to take on some of my fellow-artistes, and soon I was winning and losing half-crowns and thoroughly enjoying it. Life was wonderful and even when the audiences in the theatre at night were unco-operative and hard to please, the thought of getting out on the course the next morning would carry me through the hard work on the stage.

One of the characters I played with was a comic named Jack Wynne. Jack was a cunning old devil. He rarely played in a competition and thus preserved a handicap of fourteen which was as genuine as a six-pound treasury note. He smoked a pipe which never left his lips for the whole of the round, and he took his game very seriously. I remember on one occasion we were playing a strange course and Jack was lining up his second shot, but he kept on changing his stance and turning gradually anti-clockwise to get a straight shot at the ball. Finally I said, 'Oh come on, Jack, for heaven's sake hurry up, it's getting dark!' 'I can't yet,' yelled Jack. 'The flag keeps moving.' You couldn't blame him really. It transpired that the red flag Jack was trying to line up with was attached to the stern end of a barge that was passing by on a neighbouring canal. Somehow Jack managed to find the green, and as he lined up his putt, there was a silence that could almost be heard, if you get what I mean. Jack would brook no interference or noise of any kind, and I knew this and I was trying not to breathe as I held a passing butterfly lightly by its wings. Slowly Jack took back his putter and as he was about to stroke the ball into the hole, a stentorian voice came from the barge shouting, 'Come on, mate, for *Gawd's sake 'it it.*' Not surprisingly, Jack jerked his putt and missed the hole by at least a foot. Then for the first time in his life his pipe fell from his mouth, and he flung his putter to the ground. Pointing heatedly at the grinning bargee, he looked at me and said, 'How can a man play this game with bleedin' sailors shouting at him!'

Golf was growing. There was no doubt about it. The essential part of a comic's equipment was a drainpipe bag with six or seven clubs of assorted vintages. You would see a brassie, two cleeks, a mid-iron, a 'lofter', and a putter, piled up with the scenery and the wardrobe baskets, all atop the theatrical lorry on its way to the railway station for new theatres and unexplored golf courses. Being comic funsters by adoption, and at heart, these wonderful contemporaries of mine would introduce such funny ideas that you could never dream of.

Jimmy Lee, who has been 'straight' man for many of our star comedians, has, I think, more fun in his body than many of them put together. Who else would carry an authorized metal signpost in his golf bag which reads 'Ground under repair'? Jimmy could be in a rough that would scare the life out of a Bengal Tiger, and he would shout, 'Ground under repair,' and triumphantly hold up the metal sign to prove it. Well, that's better than the 'leather mashie' ... a side kick out of the rough with the shoe or the 'hand-iron' (throwing the ball out of a bunker by hand) and of course, Jimmy did it in sight and for all to see ... otherwise it wouldn't have been funny.

For a long time, wee Charlie Naughton of the 'Crazy Gang' held the record for the longest drive at a course in Nottingham. The hole was 498 yards long. Little Charlie sliced his ball on to the macadam roadway, and it bounced on and on and on, finally coming back on to the course twenty yards from the green. A drive of 470 yards. The mind boggles! Charlie didn't keep the record for long. Someone hit his ball right across the railway tracks and into a cattle truck on a train. The drive was measured at 263 miles. Marvellous. But what a long walk to play your second shot!

There have been lots of practical jokes too. Before the advent of 'golf trolleys' we all carried our own golf bags. I remember turning up for a competition feeling as fit as my own fiddle, and sure that I was the potential winner. I started off well, and really had the feeling that I was going to win. My score was good too. Sadly, I began to feel tired about the fourteenth and after going out in 39, I came back 5, 6, 5, 5, 6, 8, 9, 11. It wasn't until two days later that I discovered that some joker had put a fourteen-pound weight at the bottom of my golf bag. I never found out who did it. And it doesn't matter really. *The game's the thing*, and Sybil never did like having to clean those small EPNS replica cups.

Practical jokes were frequent in Show-Biz golf. The gifted cartoonist Roy Ullyett came back from America and gave me a Japanese golf ball with which to drive myself in, as captain of my club. What the onlookers didn't know was that the golf ball was explosive, and as I took my drive it took off like a jet plane with flames and blue smoke spurting out of its tail. What a laugh that caused. The boy who carried my clubs was standing just inside an out-of-bounds marker post, where he knew I was almost certain to place the shot and he was the first caddie to retrieve the ball for the traditional quid. He grabbed the ball, but he quickly dropped it again—it was still red-hot!

Perhaps the greatest of the practical jokers were the Egbert Brothers. They were in some theatrical digs where the food was terrible and the beds rock-hard, and they had to think of a scheme to get out. On the Monday night, returning from the theatre, Albert took off his shoes and socks, and stuck his feet up the chimney, and covered them with soot. He and Seth then did a hand balance, when Albert, upside down, 'walked' all over the ceiling. The next morning they brought in the landlady and told her that they could stay no longer in a house that was obviously haunted!

The boys had a great gag for the golf course, which they perpetrated on several occasions. Seth had some balls blown out of fine glass, and painted them white. He would place one on the tee-peg and as he struck it, it disintegrated and disappeared. Brother Albert would exclaim, 'Great shot Seth!' and their opponents would say, 'Where did it go?' 'Straight down the middle,' Seth would reply, and he would walk about 300 yards down the fairway and surreptitiously drop a ball down the inside of his trouser leg shouting, 'Here it is.' No wonder the opposition were astounded when they saw a little man with a half swing 'outdriving' most professional golfers.

I had reason to remember these great practical jokers. We were performing at an after-golfing impromptu concert one evening, and Seth announced that we would have an informal harmonica orchestra. Drawing me aside he handed me six mouth-organs and whispered, 'Five of these are filled with bitter aloes. Hand them out and here's yours.'

I duly inveigled five unsuspecting members on to the platform and handed out to them their cellophone-wrapped harmonicas. We began to play and mine was the only one that had been treated with bitter aloes.

If there's a lesson to be learned it is that you must never let it get you down.

Ernest Marconi, a great little Italian-American clown, got to nine handicap. But Ernest took the game very seriously. He was *too* Ernest! He didn't swear when he made a bad shot. He just bit his forearm and drew blood. It's true! Once he started 4, 3, 4, and then came to a lake hole. His first shot dropped into the water. The next one joined it. The third followed suit. Ernie then *smiled* at his partner. Yes, smiled . . . then, still smiling, Ernie walked to the edge of the lake and quietly and deliberately he threw the bag and clubs, and the shooting-stick-umbrella that his friends had bought him, deep into the water. His golf jacket, waterproof trousers, and mackintosh cap followed suit. I never saw him again, but I never go to the United States without looking for him. He'll be easy to identify. All I have to find is a little Italian-American who is smiling and doesn't play golf. And his arms will have teeth marks from the wrist to the elbow.

No! In spite of Ernie's disenchantment with the game, I am willing to bet that he is still knocking the little ball about somewhere, because the great fascination about golf is that it brings you back to the scene of your triumphs or disasters, and it is the Panacea for all our ills. At least, this is what one believes.

Like the evening at the Queen's Hotel in Birmingham, where Kenneth and George, the Western Brothers, and myself were sitting in the lounge relaxing (if you will pardon the expression) with large scotches and soda until the early hours of the morning. Kenneth thought, and rightly so, that it wouldn't be a bad idea to go to his bed when the night-porter asked him to lift up his feet while he vacuumed the carpet. George and I continued to reminisce, until the cold light of another day filtered through the curtained windows.

'Tell you what, Ted,' mused George. 'Let's go to Sandwell Park and have nine holes.' 'Great,' I said, and we got a taxi and were driven out to West Bromwich. Surprisingly, the locker-room was open even at that early hour, and we found our clubs which we had left there the previous day, and made our wayward way to the first tee. I don't know the species of bird-life that is awake at five o'clock in the morning in the environs of Birmingham, but they must have been astonished to see George Western, still attired in full evening dress, preparing to swing his driver on the first tee!

He took a practice swing and fell flat on his face. 'That's enough of that,' muttered George as I helped him up. The kindly

122

steward gave us tomato juice and Worcester Sauce and by 6 am George and I were back in our rooms at the Queen's Hotel, and fast asleep. That must surely have been the shortest game of golf on record.

Billy Bennett, who billed himself as 'Almost a Gentleman', was the fastest thing I ever saw on a golf course. If you played with Bill it was best to wear running pumps. Appearing on the same programme with him in Middlesbrough one week was another Bill from Liverpool, one Billy Matchett. 'I shan't wait,' said Bennett the evening before their golfing date. 'If you're not at the stage door by eight o'clock, I'm off.' Matchett was there at 7.30 am and away they went.

'He *ran* round,' Billy Matchett told me later. 'He could win an Olympic medal.' 'What was his score?' I inquired. 'Score?' replied Matchett. 'He doesn't bother about his score. Every time he found a bunker he kicked the ball out on to the fairway, if I sliced one two yards into the rough he said, "We'll never find that," and we gave each other every putt over six yards.'

It appears that after a quick one at the nineteenth hole, Billy Bennett took Matchett back to his (Bennett's) digs and the landlady, who had been told to prepare an early lunch, came in with a small leg of lamb, sprouts, and potatoes, and a huge dish of rice pudding. Matchett sat there in silence as Billy Bennett proceeded to demolish the lot. He then threw himself on to the bed, loosened the buttons round his waist, and said, 'Now I'll have a quick "kip". You go back to your digs and be here at half past one . . . we're going to the pictures!'

Jerry Lewis is a great comic. He's also an eccentric. Even on the course. Nearly all the Americans make for Wentworth when they come to London. The fame of the great Burma Road Golf Course has gone right around the world, and handicappers from scratch to twenty-four can't wait to put their ability against that wonderful course near Virginia Water. By the way did you ever hear such a beautiful name? I think if I had a daughter, I would have called her that.

Back to the first tee where Jerry Lewis is waiting, and he was. One of the four had failed to put in an appearance so the comedian offered to play the better ball of his opponents. The only stipulation he made was that they would concede him any putt that was less than the length of his putter. It was agreed and stakes were mentioned and believe me those Americans don't fool around. It is said that once at Thunderbird someone tried to stop the great Snead as he was on his way to the first tee! 'Sorry,' shouted Sam, 'can't stop ... there's a rich amateur waiting for me on the first and he's got a fast backswing and a pocketful of dollars.'

Jerry Lewis and the other two had quite a game. On the eighteenth green Lewis had a putt of some eight feet for the match. 'Conceded, this one?' he asked. 'Wait a minute, Jerry,' protested one of his opponents. 'That's not less than the length of your putter.' 'Why, man, it sure is,' grinned Lewis, and he proceeded to pull out the extension from the end of the club that made it at least twelve feet long. 'And you know something?' he said. 'If I put a plastic cup on the end of that, I can drag balls out of ditches.'

Some of the music halls that have been torn apart and flattened by the Bulldozers' Crunches have been unregretted by me. These are the ones in which I 'Died the Death', as they say. I wonder why they were called 'music halls'. In the main, the music was not memorable, and most of the jokes unremembered by the audiences. Most of the brave army of 'stand-up' comedians just hoped that they themselves had good memories and prayed that the customers hadn't!

'Tis said that the great Jack Benny was playing a fashionable nightclub in Las Vegas, and a fan in the bar chided Jack for having cracked several gags that he had been using for some time. Benny gave him that blank stare, and reputedly, that is all Jack ever gave. Not true, of course. Benny who built his career on the 'gimmick' of being mean, was in fact, one of the most generous comics who ever lived.

However, Jack took the barfly into the room and to a ringside table where a chubby little tourist was dining happily with his wife. Well, anyway, *somebody's* wife! 'Good evening,' said Jack. 'Enjoy the show?' The little man, beaming, said, 'Yes, it was great.' 'Fine,' said Jack, laconically. 'And which joke did you enjoy the most?' The little man replied, 'Well, do you know, I can't remember any of them!'

Well, this is how comedians survive. It has been said that there are only ten original jokes and all the others are permutations and re-creations. I can well believe it. They are like the Commandments; as Moses said when asked what the Lord had said to him when he went up the Mountain, 'Keep taking the tablets.' We are all disciples. I am thinking of the week when I was appearing on the same bill at the Empire, Newcastle, as Scott Sanders. Now Scott Sanders was a very funny man. He cracked jokes like 'I was in Dublin on the night that the Distillery burst. In ten minutes you couldn't buy a sponge in the town, it must have been a religious city. I have never seen so many men on their knees in my life.'

Now on the same bill there was an act called 'Payne and Glass'. Would you believe that? Frank Payne and Harry Glass. The mind boggles! Anyway, one morning Frank Payne said to Scott, 'Why don't you get up in the morning and come out with us and have some fresh air?' 'What are you talking about?' asked Sanders. 'Well, you know,' replied Frank. 'Come out to the golf course and have a game.' 'Golf?' queried Scott. 'What's that?' 'That's for Nits ... for Nuts.' So they persuaded him to join them, and this was at the City of Newcastle Golf Club. We duly arrived at the first tee. Payne and Glass, Ted Ray and Scott Sanders. The friendly pro fixed up Scott with a bag and a few clubs, we tossed up for partners and I got Scott, a man who had never hit a golf ball in his life. That's the kind of luck I get. If they were sawing a woman in half, I'd get the part that eats!

Scott took a deep breath. 'Great,' he said. 'This is the life ... it's marvellous.' 'Now stand back,' said Harry Glass, 'just watch me and I'll show you what to do.' Now Scott, like so many beginners, had no idea of where to stand and he couldn't have been more than three feet immediately behind Glass who took a rapid backswing and the head of his club struck the unfortunate Sanders right in the centre of the forehead, and felled him to the ground as if he had been pole-axed. Five minutes later, Scott was in the clubhouse, slowly coming back to life with a large brandy in his hand and a lump like a pigeon's egg between his temples. Half an hour later he was back in bed in his hotel. 'Golf,' he said to me that evening, 'is for Nits and Nuts ... especially *Nuts*.'

Golf is a great leveller. Poor Freddie Mills, who was to die so tragically, could never propel the wee ball very far. He appeared on the course one day and I invited him to have a go at the game. With a left hook that could have felled an ox he took a mighty swing and hit the ball a distance of some 100 yards and was amazed when a little girl whom he could have picked up with one hand sent the ball twice as far.

It's such a deceptive game and it always looks so easy to the uninitiated. Horatio Nicholls, who was really Lawrence Wright, and the composer of such world-wide hits as 'Babette' and 'Shepherd of the Hills', decided to take a highlands holiday in Scotland. He took along Joe Gilbert, himself no mean songsmith. They registered in a famous golfing hotel, and decided to have a crack at the Royal and Ancient game. They went to the pro's shop and bought the lot. New clubs, bags, and golf balls. They also hired two knowledgeable Scots caddies to pilot them around. One can imagine the feelings of the latter worthies, as they watched the pathetic attempts of the two tyros to make contact with the ball. Two hours and seven holes later, Lawrie and Joe were exhausted. Lawrie breathed heavily. 'Can you play this stupid game?' he asked his caddie. 'Och aye,' replied the bag-carrier. 'Everyone in Scotland can play golf.' 'Right,' said Lawrie. 'You get on with it and I'll watch.' Joe Gilbert was not slow to follow suit. The four completed the round with the caddies playing, and Joe and Lawrence Wright carrying the bags and having side-bets on the result!

Will Fyffe, one of the finest comedians Scotland ever produced, was a first-class angler, but never succeeded in mastering the game of golf. Whenever I visited Scotland, Bill was there with a car to pilot me to Loch Leven to fish for trout, which were plump and pink as salmon. The ghillies or boatmen would be ready and waiting, and all completely equipped. One heaved a case of beer and a couple of bottles of Scotch into the boat and the other boy carried a loaf of bread. 'Isn't that nice?' said Will. 'He's even remembered the wee birds.' As an angler, Bill was supreme. As a golfer? Don't call *us*, *we'll* call *you*! We were playing at a course not far from Glasgow and after a few holes Will called it a day. 'Come here, laddie,' he ordered his golfing ghillie. 'Yon stream, d'ye think there'll be any fish in it?' 'Aye,' came the reply, 'I've seen some big yins taken' oot o' there.' 'Fine,' said Bill, and from his tweed hat he extracted one of the fishing flies that was hooked into the wool, fastened it expertly to a length of twine that he took from his pocket, attached the end of it to his golf club and spent the rest of the morning fishing happily while the three of us finished our round of golf.

28. THE NINETEENTH—PLUS ONE

If there is one thing that the Game of Golf has taught me, it is Tolerance, for Tolerance I think is the greatest quality a man can possess. It is like that important little pause at the top of the backswing . . . it gives you time to think before you act. When I first took up the game, I was like so many others, impatient, frustrated and angry with myself when I made a poor shot. Some of the golf clubs I have flung would not have disgraced a javelin thrower in the Olympics. I don't throw clubs any more. I have become more tolerant of my failures and, besides, I can't hurl them as far as I used to!

As one gets a little older, one becomes more set in one's ways. I know I am. I don't want things to change. But it's hopeless of course. Time moves on and *we* don't change, *life* changes *us*. The varnished wooden lockers in the changing-room have been replaced by metal cubicles. Indeed sometimes it's difficult to find a hook on which to hang a jacket.

When first I joined my club, the nineteenth was an oak-panelled bar with a little partitioned-off 'snug' that accommodated just four golfers who could raise their tankards and have a friendly post-mortem on the round of golf that had just been played, and as we were nearly always the first four to tee off, we almost had 'rights'.

Now the 'snug' has gone, and so has the oak-panelled bar. The framed water-colour pictures of former captains lie in some seldom-used cupboard to become veneered with the dust of memory. Only one memento remains. It's an oval-shaped brass plate that has been there from the first day that the club was formed. It's under the bar clock and I read the inscription whenever I check the time to see if I'm due to go home and join Sybil for lunch.

It reads simply 'DRINK DOWN ALL UNKINDNESS', and I suppose that's as good a philosophy as any.